COME TO THE FEAST

Come to the Feast

SEEKING GOD'S BOUNTY
FOR OUR LIVES AND SOULS

Marchiene Vroon Rienstra

William B. Eerdmans Publishing Company
Grand Rapids, Michigan / Cambridge, U.K.

© 1995 Wm. B. Eerdmans Publishing Co.
255 Jefferson Ave. S.E., Grand Rapids, Michigan 49503 /
P.O. Box 163, Cambridge CB3 9PU U.K.

Printed in the United States of America

00 99 98 97 96 95   7 6 5 4 3 2 1

Library of Congress Cataloging-in-Publication Data

Rienstra, Marchiene Vroon, 1941-
Come to the feast: seeking God's bounty for our lives and souls /
Marchiene Vroon Rienstra.
p.   cm.
Includes bibliographical references.
ISBN 0-8028-0822-0 (paper: alk. paper)
1. Spiritual life — Christianity. I. Title.
BV4501.2.R526 1995
248.4 — dc20   95-34034
CIP

Contents

Acknowledgments

I dedicate this book to all the companions at the Feast who tried out the foods described in this book with me while I was pastor of Hope Church in Holland, Michigan, and was teaching at Western Seminary; and to those companions who over the years have come to me for spiritual direction and have nourished me with their love, trust, and open sharing.

I am especially grateful to my friends Len VanderZee and Neva Evenhouse for their thoughtful and encouraging response to the first draft of this manuscript; and to Ron and Deb Rienstra, my son and daughter-in-law, whose careful and helpful suggestions made this a much better book.

Finally, I am grateful once again for the positive support and encouragement of Jon Pott and Ina Vondiziano at Eerdmans Publishing Company, and for the sensitive and fine editing of Mary Hietbrink, whose work on this book has brought it to a healthy birth.

Introduction

"Come to the feast."

These welcome words of invitation resound again and again in the Bible, summoning one and all to come to the Banqueting Table prepared by God for their nourishment and pleasure. The ordinary and universal human act of eating good food together becomes a powerful metaphor for spiritual nourishment provided by God as the host.

"This image of the banquet remains, throughout the whole Bible, the central image of life. It is the image of life at its creation and also the image of life at its end and fulfillment: '. . . that you eat and drink at My table,'" says Alexander Schmemann in his book entitled *For the Life of the World*.

In the very beginning, God creates a garden in Eden with plants and fruit trees to provide food for Adam and Eve. Paradise is a place of feasting and gladness.

Much later, when God frees the people of Israel from slavery and establishes laws to guide them in being a "light to the nations," chief among those laws is the command to "keep the feast" — not just one feast, but many: the Passover Feast, the Feast of Tabernacles, the Feast of the Firstfruits, the Harvest Feasts, and the feasts for the new moon and for the full moon.

The writers of the Psalms often reflect on their experience of feasting from God's abundance, sensing its spiritual dimension. "You have put more joy in my heart than those whose grain and wine abound" (4:7). "You have prepared a table before me in the presence of my enemies" (23:5).

"Wisdom has prepared her table," says Proverbs 9, "and sent out her maids to call from the highest places in the town . . . 'Come, eat of my bread and drink of the wine I have mixed. Forsake foolishness, and live, and walk in the way of insight'" (vv. 2-3, 5-6).

The prophet echoes the divine invitation: "Ho, everyone who thirsts, come to the waters; and you who have no money, come . . . eat! . . . Hearken diligently to me, and eat what is good, and delight yourselves in fatness" (Isa. 55:1-2). He peers far into the future and sees a great feast in the making: "On this mountain the Lord of hosts will make for all peoples a feast of rich food, a feast of well-aged wines" (25:6).

When Jesus comes, he comes eating and drinking, feasting with "publicans and sinners," and telling story after story about banquets. He tells us that God is like a waiting father who prepares a wonderful feast for his lost son upon his return home (Luke 15). He teaches us that the kingdom of heaven is like a great feast to which a king has invited many people. When they refuse to come because other things are more important to them, the king brings in people both good and bad from the streets and fills the banqueting hall with guests (Matt. 22). At the Last Supper, which becomes the church's feast in memory of Christ's death and resurrection, Jesus looks ahead to the time when he will drink the fruit of the vine with his followers in his Abba's kingdom (Matt. 26).

This wonderful image of the feast, which weaves its way throughout the Bible, is the foundation for the early Christian phrase "the Banqueting Table of the Lamb," a metaphor that expresses the fulfillment of all things, when God's will is done on earth as it is in heaven, and all creation is made new. But the generous provision that the Banqueting Table of God makes for our spiritual nourishment is also and already available to us here and now. We don't have to wait until we get to heaven or until the reign of God is established on earth. In fact, feasting at the Banqueting Table can be a "heavenly" experience that is part of our everyday lives.

Because this is a truth I have personally come to experience, I am eager to share the sustenance I have received at the Banqueting Table with others who are spiritually hungry. In my life as a pastor, seminary teacher, spiritual director, and friend, I have found that there are still many Christians who are not aware of the rich and varied fare that God has provided for the nourishment of their souls and lives. Their background and experience have exposed them to only a small part of the Feast that is available to them. As a result, some of them have suffered unnecessarily from spiritual malnourishment. I have found it very satisfying to share my discoveries of "soul food" with these people, and to see how they flourish as a result. In fact, that's why I have written this book: it gives me a way to share the bounty of the Feast with many more of those who hunger and thirst, in the hope that they will "taste and see the goodness of God," and find at the Banqueting Table more than enough to satisfy their souls, both now and forever.

How to Use
Come to the Feast

You may simply choose to read through this book as you would any other. But I've written it in such a way that you can also use it with a friend or a group. Specific "spiritual exercises" are included at the end of each chapter to help you experience what you've read and integrate the material into your life. You can do the exercises alone, of course, or you can use them as the basis for discussion with others.

One church group I know used a rough draft of this book for its semimonthly meetings from fall to spring. Each month they read a chapter together aloud at one meeting, worked through the exercises at home during the next two weeks, and then discussed their experience with and reflection on the exercises at the next meeting. Using this method, they covered a chapter and its corresponding exercises every month, and they made their way through the book from September through May (roughly the church year). Of course, there are many other ways to use the book, and I urge you to explore which one might be best for you.

At the end of each chapter I've also included a short list of books that will flesh out and clarify the chapter's content in a significant way. The list provides brief descriptions of these books to help you decide which ones you might want to read for yourself. You can order them by title and author from most bookstores, and you can find some of them in a well-stocked library. If you are studying this book with a group, you might want to pool your resources so that you can jointly buy some of the recommended books and share them with each other.

If you choose to work through the exercises at the end of each chapter, I recommend that you write down your responses and reflections in a journal. It will give you a good way to be focused in your reflections, and it will be invaluable to you as a record of your spiritual development.

PART ONE

CHAPTER 1

The Worship of the Church

Let's say that you have received an invitation from God to come to a marvelous banquet of spiritual nourishment. The Feast is ready. You have decided to accept the invitation. You have taken time from the obligations of your life to come to the Banqueting Table, because there's an empty ache deep inside you that you realize might be spiritual hunger. And besides, you're a little curious too. What is this feast for the soul like? What sort of food has God provided?

The main course at the Banqueting Table is the worship that has been developed through the ages by the Spirit of God, through the people of God. All who come into the church, or are born into it and grow up in it, are provided with this rich spiritual food for the nourishment of their souls. But many are unaware of the richness of meaning in the worship of the church. It is so familiar that they simply go through the motions without realizing what is there to nourish them personally.

I myself did that for quite a long while. Although worship often inspired me, I didn't realize until I was in seminary what good nourishment it provided for my soul. I had never before understood that it literally taught me how to pray and how to live. When I realized what I had been missing, worship became much more of a feast for my soul.

In order that your soul may also feast when you worship with God's people, let me share with you what I have learned.

If you attend worship regularly in a church that has a classic pattern, you are taking in great wisdom about how to pray and live as a Christian.

You begin with words and songs of praise. To praise God is a sure way to enter into a lively sense of God's presence and goodness. Prayer that begins with praise lifts us out of our narrow and often self-centered concerns, and refills our souls with the spirit of joy and celebration, which is one of God's greatest gifts to us. Praise is like a wind fanning the spark of our faith into a blazing flame. When we center our attention on the goodness, the love, and the saving power of God rather than on our troubles and the problems of the world, we are able to lift our heads high in hope, and our rags of sorrow are exchanged for garments of gladness.

The pattern of worship teaches us to always begin our prayer with praise. "Enter God's presence with gladness, and come into God's courts with praise," says Psalm 100. This applies to our everyday prayer as well as to our weekly prayer in the assembly of God's people. How much better off we would be if we trained ourselves to begin every day with words and songs of praise to God as we rose, showered, dressed, and prepared for the day. We would realize that there is always something for which we can praise God, and that doing so washes the grime of grumbling from the windows of our souls so we can see more clearly.

The worship of the church teaches us the importance of praise not only in our relationship with God but also in our daily life and our personal relationships with other people. Consider how our daily meetings with others would be transformed if they began with expressions of mutual praise and appreciation. So often we take others for granted, especially those closest to us. We think as much or more about their faults as we do about their virtues and gifts. But worship teaches us to always begin with praise and words of appreciation.

In the same way, worship teaches us to respond with a spirit of praise in all of life's circumstances. This doesn't mean that we should adopt a Pollyannish attitude that keeps us from seeing things realistically. Nor does it imply that we should exude a syrupy, sentimental sweetness or wear a phony smile. But it does challenge our faith. Do we really believe that in everything God works for good with those who love God and know themselves called according to God's purposes, and that absolutely nothing can separate us from the love of God? (Rom. 8:28, 38-39). Then we can rejoice always, and in everything give God thanks and praise (1 Thess. 5:16, 18). Worship teaches us to do this, and doing this strengthens our faith and lifts our hearts, just as well-seasoned and well-prepared food strengthens the body and delights the taste. The difference praise gives us in any and all of life's situations is like the difference between viewing something from a dark, shadowed valley and from the sunlit peak of a mountaintop. It makes a big difference where we stand. Worship and prayer and living that is permeated with praise put us on the mountaintop.

After praising God in worship, you probably join in a prayer of confession in which you acknowledge, with others, the shadows in your life, in the church, and in the world. To do this frequently, with honesty and openness, fosters the foundational virtue of humility in the Christian life. As we become conscious of the holy light of God's presence, we are able to see more clearly our limits, our needs, our griefs, our wounds, and our guilt. We don't have to pretend to be something we're not. Of course, God already knows what is wrong with us and the world. But *we* need to see and confess it before one another. We are all wounded and wounding, in need of God's healing and forgiveness. If we took our act of confession really seriously, we wouldn't wear the masks we often do in the Christian community. This act of worship gives us permission to be real with each other. It is a blessed relief, if we will only take advantage of it.

Our confession to and honesty with ourselves, others, and God opens us up to receive the assurance of God's pardon and the gift of the amazing grace that God is always more ready to give than we are to receive. Like the prodigal son, we can run into the open arms of God's tender love and there find all the comfort and acceptance we need. In fact, if we have the eyes to see it, we will realize that God is running down the road to meet us every time we turn toward home, leaving behind our self-imposed exile and alienation.

Through this act of reconciliation, the worship of God's

people teaches us that our own prayer needs to include both praise and confession, the acknowledgment of grace and of guilt, of joy and of sorrow. There can be no wholeness for us without honesty and humility. We must not avoid looking at our own dark side. But neither are we to wallow in guilt. The purpose of confession is to help us realize our need to once again turn in God's direction and run into the loving arms always open for us. However unworthy we may feel, God is always ready to robe us in forgiveness and kill the fatted calf of celebration for our homecoming. Our part is to desire to serve God and to live in the house of God's presence as a beloved daughter or son.

Of course, the act of confession, repentance, and reconciliation in worship also teaches us how important it is to realize our faults and ask for forgiveness in our relationships with others. When we say "I was wrong. I'm sorry. Please forgive me. I won't do it again," and truly mean it, we are offering the balm that heals the wounds we often inflict on others, knowingly and unknowingly. Perhaps this act of humility on our part would be easier if we would enter more wholeheartedly into confession when we worship, and when we pray by ourselves, being as open and specific as possible.

Conversely, when someone asks us for forgiveness and wants to make a fresh start in a relationship, we cannot refuse if we pray and worship with integrity. How can we, who have been forgiven so much so often by God, refuse to forgive another who humbly confesses his or her fault and asks for forgiveness and the chance to make it right? It is important, of course, that the act of repentance be real, whether on our part or the other person's part. The Gospels make it clear that true repentance is shown by certain fruits, such as Zacchaeus's promise to restore fourfold all that he had cheated others of as a tax collector. The words of confession become a sham if they are not accompanied by deeds that reveal a genuine change of mind and heart in the right direction.

Having been reconciled to God through the act of confession, we are ready to hear God speak to us, as if we were little children at our Mother's Breast (Ps. 131). Whether or not the sermon is "good," we can always get some nourishment from the Scriptures when they are read and explained. If our hearts are open like a little child's, we

6

will receive something — perhaps just a word or a phrase or an insight to integrate into our lives, or a question to ponder during the week. If we pray for the Holy Spirit's illumination in and through the proclaimed Word, we will not be disappointed.

Our open-hearted listening to God in worship teaches us to listen to God in our daily and personal prayer. Worship and prayer are much more than our speaking to God. There must be "equal time" for God to speak to us. After all, whose words are most important? The worship of the church teaches us to feed our souls on what God says to us by setting aside a time of quiet when we read Scripture or other devotional material, or simply listen in silence for God's "still, small voice" within.

When we learn to listen to God, we realize how important it is to really listen to other people in our daily lives. Many psychologists and psychiatrists say their offices are filled with a steady stream of clients in part because these hard-pressed and troubled people have not been able to find others who will really listen to them with love and patience. Such listening is demanding, just as really listening to a sermon is. It means putting our own agenda on the back burner, biting our lips when we want to interject opinions and advice, and simply hearing the other person out, without judgment. God certainly listens to us in this way. Can we return the favor? There is very little we can do for another that is more valuable than genuine, open-hearted listening.

After we have listened to God in worship, we usually participate in a confession of our faith. "Faith comes from hearing the Word of God," say the Scriptures, and so we respond to the proclamation of the Word in words that express the faith of the Christian community. Sometimes the words are traditional, like those of the Apostles' Creed. Sometimes they are contemporary — perhaps those of a recent confession written for a particular denomination or a particular congregation. Sometimes they are expressed in a hymn or a Psalm. In any case, the worship of the church teaches us that the first and proper response to God's speaking to us is the response of faith. We believe what God has said. We trust God's truth and direction for our lives. And we join our hearts and voices with other Christians in proclaiming the faith that binds us together.

In this way, the worship of the church teaches us to proclaim our faith in our daily lives as well as when we are gathered together as a congregation. This too is food for our souls. Nothing strengthens our faith more than expressing it to others. Our faithful witness to our trust in God and to our belief in God's truth is meant to be a vital part of our lives. Even if the best we can say is "I believe — Lord, help my unbelief!" we are still confessing what we can — and that is far better than not confessing our faith at all.

Moreover, we learn from our worship how important it is to declare our faith in others as well. What relationship can flourish without trust? And as experience teaches us quite plainly, we can bring out the best in other people by letting them know that we have faith in them, believe in them, and trust them to be the best they can be. Like praise, confession, and listening, the expression of our faith and trust is essential not only to worship but also to our relationships, if they are to be as rich and as mutually rewarding as they can be.

After we confess our faith together in worship, we offer our gifts and prayers to God. In many churches, this is an integral part of holy communion as well. In fact, it is often called "eucharist," meaning "sacrifice of thanks."

When we offer gifts of money, we are reminded that an essential part of our prayer and life is the grateful offering of our time, our abilities, and our gifts in the service of God and others. The worship of God and an authentic prayer life include acts of devotion, sacrifice, and service. These are not separate from or a result of prayer and worship, as many think. They *are* prayer and worship. Preparing a meal for others, giving money for food for the hungry, working politically for housing for the homeless — all these and countless other acts are offerings in a life that is lived worshiping God.

The prayers of petition and intercession that accompany the offering of our gifts in worship reveal the close tie between what we ask of God and what *we* are willing to do to make our prayers come true. Sometimes when we pray we seem to assume that it is entirely up to God to bring peace on earth, feed the hungry, heal the sick, take care of people we love, and so on. Of course, all this is ultimately in God's hands, and one of the main reasons to pray about what concerns us is that it is a way of casting all our burdens on God, who cares for us and what concerns us more passionately than we can imagine. In fact, it does us no good at all — and is arrogant besides — to attempt to carry the burden of the world's ills, or even the ills afflicting people we care about, on our shoulders.

But we can leave the burden with God and still do our fair share to help those whom we pray for and respond to the problems of the world as best we can. We offer ourselves along with our intercessory prayers, and we ask God to guide us in doing what we need to do. This is never more than we can handle. All we need to realize is that the *results* of our giving and praying and acting need to be left in God's hands. Our part is to simply do the giving and praying and acting as God guides us, so that our weekly worship spills over into our daily lives, and they become an offering to God.

The offering of our gifts and prayers also reminds us that all we are and have is a gift from God, and that our whole lives are to be a gift of grateful response for all God's goodness to us. The prayers of petition and intercession teach us to pray and care in a heartfelt way for the whole world, the whole church, and the people in our lives. Such prayer keeps us mindful that we live in human community and owe a debt of love to all who are given to us. Through the prayer of God's people, we come to share in God's perspective and God's love for all creatures and all creation.

The final act of worship, after the offering and prayers, is the benediction, which means the blessing of God. This is the last word — of the worship service and of our lives. In the Bible, to bless someone means to give the gifts of affirmation, resources, and empowerment for an abundant life. This is what God does when we receive the benediction. It is the blessing of God that empowers us and makes our lives fruitful. We are never without it: we can count on God's blessing to accompany us through every hour of every day.

Thus we learn that our worship and prayer are crowned with God's blessing, and that to live in God's presence is a blessing. And just as God blesses us, we too can bless others. In one family I know, for instance, the parents always give a blessing to their children at the door when they leave for school. A minister I know always gives the benediction to each person she calls on, laying her hands on the individual's head as she repeats the benediction that is used in worship. There are many ways we can also "give the benediction" to others and be a blessing to them. Worship teaches us to do so.

In all the movements of worship we have examined, we learn how to pray and how to live. Our souls are fed with food that nourishes us when we attend closely to what is happening when we meet with God's people to worship. What is even more wonderful is that there are so many ways the food at God's Banqueting Table is prepared, seasoned, and served. In the richly varied types of worship that have developed throughout the church universal, there is something for everyone.

The profound silence and simple speaking at a Quaker meeting; the exuberant singing, movement, and preaching in African-American worship; the stately rituals and robes, incense and icons of Eastern Orthodox worship — all the worship of Christians in the great variety of cultures and denominations that exist in the world today are part of the Feast to which we are invited. To explore the abundance of different foods at the Table is very much like being at an ethnic food festival!

Unfortunately, a great many Christians do not partake of the variety that is available to them. While it is good to worship regularly in the tradition and with the congregation of our choice, we impoverish ourselves if we never take the time and opportunity to worship with Christians who have a very different style from the one we are most accustomed to.

I and many others find that there is something in our souls that resonates with Baptist, Pentecostal, Presbyterian, Catholic, Orthodox, and Quaker worship. It is as if our souls are too hungry to be satisfied with any single denomination or style of worship. For example, there is something in the "joyful sorrow" that penetrates the glorious singing at the Russian Orthodox Easter vigil which feeds my soul as nothing else can. There is an exuberant, deep-down faith evident in the singing and preaching in African-American churches that nourishes me as nothing else does. My times of worship with Christian sisters and brothers in India and

Pakistan, Ethiopia and Nigeria, Jerusalem and Chicago have fed me in ways that worship with my home congregations could not. In the church as well as in creation, it seems that God is a lover of boundless variety. The human soul seems to flourish on such variety and wither when there is "too much of a sameness."

With such a marvelous variety of "soul food" spread before us at the Banqueting Table, why do so many Christians still complain that they don't know how to pray, or that the church doesn't feed them spiritually? What keeps people from coming to the Table and receiving the nourishment offered them there?

There are at least four problems that are important to acknowledge and understand.

The first is that many people who attend worship are simply unaware of the Feast that is set before them. They act like folks who sit down to eat a delicious meal that was meant to be savored and absentmindedly wolf down the food. Their lack of attentiveness to and appreciation of the spiritual food they are eating, and the people they are eating with, leaves them unsatisfied. Often these individuals hurry through hymns, Scripture readings, and prayers without apparent thought or feeling. There is little sense of wonder or mystery in their worship. It certainly doesn't seem like the communion of the saints — or a feast!

A second problem is the fact that in each of us there is resistance as well as attraction to the prospect of drawing closer to God and being committed to a deep spiritual journey. The community of the church often functions not only as a place where people can find God but also as a place where people can hide from God. For many people, going through the motions of religious life becomes a substitute for the authentic and vulnerable sharing of their lives in God. They accept beliefs and doctrines about God without real struggle and soul searching, and these become substitutes for a lively and growing faith that develops from a personal relationship with God. To the extent that this is true, such people often experience a kind of fear and rigidity that prevents them from getting healthy spiritual nourishment in worship.

A third problem is the narrowness and lack of inclusiveness in many church communities. Whole categories of people are not

welcomed and integrated into the worship and life of the church
— minorities, people with disabilities, people who are on the fringe
of society, single people, even children and the elderly. Their needs
are considered, if at all, in only the most superficial ways. Leadership is often not open to women. A masculine bias in the language
and tradition which subtly excludes women shapes the community.
The worship provided by many churches feels more like a fence
than an open door.

Moreover, there are ongoing divisions among churches and
denominations, based on a certain subtle arrogance and self-satis-
faction. They often compete with each other for members rather
than cooperating with each other to serve the community and the
world. They fail to realize that one congregation or denomination
cannot do everything well or serve everyone's needs. All of this
functions to keep away many who are spiritually hungry and
looking for a place of nourishment that is truly open and welcom-
ing and accepting — a place that feels like a friendly inn offering
a feast rather than a brand-name gas station that's trying to entice
customers to show up regularly for their weekly fill-up.

Fourth and finally, many church communities suffer from the
problem of emphasizing hierarchies of power, structures, objec-
tives, tasks, and programs, rather than emphasizing mutuality,
process, spontaneity, dependence on the Holy Spirit's leading, and
the cultivation of relationships that nourish spiritual growth and
health for everyone in the community. Buildings and budgets often
seem to take priority over the healing, reconciling, and nourishing
aspects of the church's life. Where this is true, the spiritual atmosphere prevents people from feasting at the Table set for them.

By the grace of God, there is at the same time a deep stream
of awareness of the depth and meaning of worship as a feast for
the soul. This awareness can be found everywhere in the church,
but especially in the Orthodox, Catholic, and Episcopal traditions.
The wonderful riches of the Holy Spirit's prayer that they have
preserved in the common prayer of the church and the saints
(despite its limits and masculine bias) are being shared with the
whole church in this ecumenical age, with renewal in many places
as the result. Moreover, the Western church is beginning to listen
to the churches of Africa, Asia, the Middle East, the island nations,

and South America. Their vitality in worship is enriching the worship of the community of believers everywhere. So are the new forms of Christian community that are coming to birth as God moves to renew the face of the earth. Pentecostal churches, house churches, small "base communities" of the poor and oppressed in the Third World, women's communities — all these and many more are providing both traditional and new foods for spiritual nourishment of the hungry.

Now the question is this: How do we take advantage of the Feast for the soul that is provided by and through the life, prayer, and weekly worship of the people of God? Of course, each one of us must find the answer to this question for himself or herself. I offer the following suggestions in the hope that one or more of them will be helpful to you. As I mentioned earlier, using a journal to record your thoughts and feelings will be beneficial.

1. Record what has nourished you in worship in the past.
2. Describe any difficulties or struggles you have had in finding good nourishment for your soul in worship.
3. Based on what you have read in this chapter, attend worship with an awareness of how it is feeding you. Reflect on and record your experience.
4. Attend worship of a kind that is not familiar to you, and reflect on and record how it nourishes you.
5. For one week, consciously let the "meat" of worship, as described in this chapter, nourish and shape your prayer and your daily life. Reflect on all the elements — praise, confession, listening, expressing faith, offering prayers and gifts and acts of love, and receiving and giving blessing. Then explain how you were able to incorporate each element of worship into your prayer and your life. (It might be helpful to focus on just one element in your prayer and life each day.)
6. Explore the Book of Common Prayer of the Episcopal Church or other guides for daily prayer now available in many denominational hymnbooks and prayer books. They contain the "meat" of the worship of God's people through the ages, modified for contemporary and personal use. Many churches have these books in their libraries, and they can also be

13

ordered from religious bookstores. Try using one or more of these daily prayer models for your personal prayer, and reflect on your experience in your journal. (You might want to try using one of the guides for morning and evening prayer for at least a week.)

Books for Further Reference

1. *For the Life of the World: Sacraments and Orthodoxy* by Alexander Schmemann
This book, written from an Eastern Orthodox viewpoint, examines human beings as essentially worshiping creatures, created to be high priests of creation. It eloquently shows the close relationship between worship and life, and the depths of spiritual meaning in both.

2. *Worship* by Evelyn Underhill
In this book, one of the foremost writers on spirituality in our century probes the spiritual depths of prayer and worship, exploring many Christian spiritual traditions and a sweep of liturgical history as she does so.

3. *The Mystery of Christ: The Liturgy as Spiritual Experience* by Thomas Keating
This is a remarkable reflection on the experience of Christ in worship that recovers a contemplative sense of the liturgical year and its capacity for shaping us into more Christ-like beings.

4. *The Book of Common Prayer* (Seabury Press)
This is a classic and helpful resource for specific prayers and worship services for the whole year. It also provides a recommended schedule for reading Scripture every morning and evening in harmony with the liturgical year.

CHAPTER 2

The Bread of Life

The Word of God is an integral part of our worship, but it should also be an integral part of our daily lives. In the Word, God provides us with essential spiritual food, which one of the great classic hymns of the church calls the Bread of Life:

> Break Thou the Bread of Life, dear Lord, to me,
> As Thou didst break the loaves beside the sea.
> Beyond the sacred page I seek Thee, Lord.
> My spirit longs for Thee, O Living Word!

If we think of the Word of God in Scripture in this way, as something to "eat" — that is, to take into our very being — we will find it a good corrective to the common, rather rationalistic way of studying the Bible that places most of the emphasis on our mental grasp of its concepts. Of course, such understanding is important. But it often does too little to speak to the heart or nourish the soul. It emphasizes words and ideas, and it is limited to a single aspect of ourselves — our minds. Often, this way of approaching Scripture becomes dry, dull, or irrelevant.

Still, Christians keep returning to Scripture, for through the centuries countless numbers of them have found it to be a powerful and living Word, bringing renewal and sparking profound conversions of heart, mind, and life. Saint Augustine had such a conversion, and he described his experience in these memorable words:

There was a little garden belonging to our lodging, of which we had the use — as of the whole house — for the master, our landlord, did not live there. The tempest in my breast hurried me out into this garden, where no one might interrupt the fiery struggle in which I was engaged with myself, until it came to the outcome that thou knewest though I did not. . . .

Now when deep reflection had drawn up out of the secret depths of my soul all my misery and had heaped it up before the sight of my heart, there arose a mighty storm, accompanied by a mighty rain of tears. . . . I was . . . weeping in the most bitter contrition of my heart, when suddenly I heard the voice of a boy or a girl — I know not which — coming from the neighboring house, chanting over and over again, "Pick it up, read it; pick it up, read it." Immediately I ceased weeping and began most earnestly to think whether it was usual for children in some kind of game to sing such a song, but I could not remember ever having heard the like. So, damming the torrent of my tears, I got to my feet, for I could not but think that this was a divine command to open the Bible and read the first passage I should light upon. For I had heard how Anthony, accidentally coming into church while the gospel was being read, received the admonition as if what was read had been addressed to him: "Go and sell what you have and give it to the poor, and you shall have treasure in heaven; and come and follow me" [Matt. 19:21]. By such an oracle he was forthwith converted to thee.

So I quickly returned to the bench where Alypius was sitting, for there I had put down the apostle's book when I had left there. I snatched it up, opened it, and in silence read the paragraph on which my eyes first fell: "Not in rioting and drunkenness, not in chambering and wantonness, not in strife and envying, but put on the Lord Jesus Christ, and make no provision for the flesh to fulfill the lusts thereof" [Rom. 13:13-14]. I wanted to read no further, nor did I need to. For instantly, as the sentence ended, there was infused in my heart something like the light of full certainty and all the gloom of doubt vanished away."[1]

---

1. Saint Augustine, excerpted from *Augustine: "Conversions" and "En-*

When Scripture functions this way in our lives, it is because we read it or hear it in an experiential way, as a direct encounter with God. We listen for the voice of God, who addresses us in and through the words of the Bible.

Of course, God's Spirit can speak to anyone through Scripture, regardless of the method or approach which that person is using. However, there is a way of remembering, or reading and reflecting on Scripture, that has been used for fifteen centuries and has proved to be a reliable and effective way to open the heart as well as the mind to Scripture. It is called *lectio divina,* which means "divine reading." It is not a study of Scripture that treats Scripture as an object to be examined; rather, it is a way of taking in Scripture — like the Bread of Life it is — so that the Word, like bread, becomes an integral part of us.

And it *is* enormously important to "eat" and "digest" the Word of God as we sit at the Table that God has prepared for the nourishment of our souls. If we merely look at or talk about the Bread of the Word, it will have little effect on our lives. But if we really take it in, our beings and our lives will be transformed.

Lectio divina as a way of taking in Scripture was pioneered and practiced by Saint Benedict and his twin sister, Saint Scholastica. Their followers, the Benedictines, have continued the practice of *lectio divina* ever since the sixth century. In fact, there are still many vital communities of Benedictine Christians in the world today, and in all of them, *lectio divina* is the foundation of their spirituality and spiritual practice.

Although there is a certain classic "technique" for doing divine reading, it is important to remember that the steps are to be learned as one learns the basic steps of a dance. Once they are practiced and mastered, they become "natural," and then one can improvise and engage in divine reading without the self-conscious attention to the steps that accompanies the early stages of learning them.

Moreover, as with the movements of the liturgy, the movements of *lectio divina* describe the whole of one's life in the Spirit

---

chiridion," vol. 7 of the Library of Christian Classics, trans. and ed. Albert C. Outler (London: SCM Press; Philadelphia: Westminster Press, 1955).

as well as a particular period and method of prayerful reading of Scripture. With this in mind, I invite you to consider the four steps of *lectio divina*.

The first step is to choose and recite the Scripture that you want to take in. You can read from the Bible according to a given plan, such as the one found in the daily readings used by the Episcopal Church, which can be found in the back of the Book of Common Prayer. Many other devotional guides for Bible reading are available from various church presses, such as the popular resources offered by The Upper Room publishing house in Nashville, Tennessee. Or, if your minister and church follow a published lectionary of readings for the Sundays of the year, such as the one found in the planning calendar of the Reformed Church of America, you can read the Scripture passages that were the basis for the sermon last Sunday or the passages that will be the basis for the sermon next Sunday.

On occasion, you can follow Saint Augustine's example and simply choose a passage spontaneously that speaks to you, or a passage that you can remember in a spirit of prayer. It is not even necessary to have a Bible with you. You may have many words of Scripture stored in your mind and heart that the Holy Spirit will help you recall if you ask.

You might also find that the Psalms, hymns, and prayers of the saints provide a rich resource for listening to God's Word. The Psalms have been the prayer book of God's people for many centuries. They truly are a staff of life, the most nourishing of breads, and the mainstay of *lectio divina* for the Benedictines as well as for millions of other Christians.

Hymns are particularly important in the Protestant tradition, and their words and music have provided rich food for the soul for many Christians. I often find that I will awake in the morning with the words of a hymn in my mind, and as I sing them in my heart before I get up, they speak to me in a way that turns out to be just what I need for the day ahead. As I have become acquainted with the prayers of the saints in such books as the *Eerdmans' Book of Famous Prayers* and the *People's Prayer Book,* I have also found a great deal of spiritual nourishment in them.

With all these kinds of bread to choose from, there is more than enough to provide for our souls. The important thing to remember is to listen to your inner response as you read or recite whatever part of the Word you have chosen. When you feel a response to a certain passage, thought, or word — when something inside you leaps or is drawn to it or pierced by it — stop, and make it your choice. For this is the Word that God is wanting to feed you. A process of this kind requires a special dual attentiveness: you need to be attentive both to the words you are reading, hearing, or recalling, and to what is happening inside you. It is usually true that "less is more": a few words or a short passage is plenty when you intend to thoroughly digest the content.

When you have chosen the Word that really speaks to you, read or repeat it aloud, slowly, perhaps several times over in order to savor its meaning in various ways. This step of saying the words out loud (or singing or chanting them if you prefer) is often neglected in modern times, for we have lost the ancient Hebrews' sense that words are physical too, and that they do not become completely real or effective until they are sounded out or spoken. The Hebrews' strong sense of this is reflected in the Hebrew Scriptures, in which God always speaks the Word out loud — indeed, God has done so from creation onward. It is likely that the Word will have greater reality for you too if you honor its physicality with your tongue, your lips, and your voice. Here the words of Psalm 51 are apt: "O Lord, open my lips, and my mouth shall proclaim your praise!" This first step of *lectio divina* is, for obvious reasons, called *lectio*, meaning "reading."

The second step is to meditate upon the Word that you have put into your mouth via *lectio*. The word *meditatio* — the Latin word from which the English word "meditation" is taken — is applied to this step. To meditate means to focus on, reflect on, and ponder something in order to enter into its depths. There are many ways to do this besides the familiar methods (lecture, question-and-answer, discussion) used in traditional Bible study.

One way is to simply and slowly repeat the words you have chosen over and over again, until you feel satisfied. This is a way of "soaking up" the Word rather than trying to figure out what it means with your mind. This is a more contemplative, receptive approach, and it works well for many people who relish some relief from the busy workings of their minds.

Another way is to use your imagination to create an image

19

or scene that relates to the Word you have chosen and then put yourself into it with as much vivid detail as possible. This is a wonderful way to meditate on Jesus' parables, for example, or on other biblical stories, sayings, or events that contain vivid images. You might also draw, paint, or model with clay the image or scene on which you are focusing, especially if you are a person who is visually oriented or drawn to art. In this way, your senses as well as your mind and imagination can be involved in the meditation. Music and dance are still other ways to meditate that can involve your body and your feelings in a profound and wonderful way. Of course, asking questions and mentally pondering the meaning of Scripture are forms of meditation too.

What is important to remember is that meditation is more effective when you involve several aspects of yourself — thinking, feeling, imagining, sensing. It is like slowly savoring what you are eating — chewing it slowly and being fully aware of its aroma, color, texture, temperature, and taste. This is a far more satisfying way to eat than the "fast food" style; and meditating in various ways in a leisurely manner is a far more satisfying way of "tasting and seeing" that God's Word is good!

When you have completed *meditatio,* you are ready to proceed to the third step, which is *oratio,* or "prayer-response." The prayer arises from your unique personal interaction with God's Word to you in *lectio* and *meditatio.* Perhaps you will be moved to respond with a prayer of praise and thanksgiving for some new insight or needed comfort God has given you. Perhaps you will be moved to a prayer of confession as you realize some specific way in which you need to be forgiven. Perhaps the Word you have taken in reveals changes you need to make, and so you will be moved to offer a prayer of petition, asking for God's help in living the Word you have eaten. Perhaps you will be reminded to pray for someone or something. Any or all of the above are ways to pray your own heartfelt response to God. You have been listening to God speak to you through the Word; now it is your turn to speak to God in response. Thus, divine reading becomes a dialogue, and Scripture changes from an object to be studied to a means of communion with God that is vivid and direct. Often it will help you concentrate if you write down your prayer, or sing it, draw it, paint it, mold it, or express it

20

through physical movement. Again, the more you focus and involve your whole self in your *oratio,* the more nourishment you will receive from the Word of God.

A famous example of *oratio* (and *lectio* and *meditatio* as well) is the advice Martin Luther gave his barber when he asked Luther how to pray. John Doberstein, author of the *Minister's Prayer Book,* gives this description of Luther's response: "Luther complied with [his barber's] request by writing this little treatise, which was published in the spring of 1535 under the title *A Simple Way to Pray, for a Good Friend.* It is counted a classic in Lutheran devotional literature. It should be noted that Luther always begins with a passage from the Bible or the [Apostles'] Creed. First he carefully reflects upon the content of the passage, then meditates [upon] what the Holy Spirit is saying to him personally in and through the passage."

Dear Master Peter:

I give you the best I have; I tell you how I myself pray. May our Lord God grant you and everyone to do better! Amen.

First, whenever I feel that I have grown cold and disinclined to pray, because of other tasks and thoughts (for the flesh and the devil always prevent and hinder prayer), I take my little Psalter, hasten into my room, or, if it is during the day and I have time, to the church where others are gathered, and begin to say the Lord's Prayer, the Ten Commandments, the Creed, and then if I have time, some words of Christ, Paul, or the Psalms, saying them quietly to myself just as children do.

Therefore, it is a good thing to let prayer be the first business of the morning and the last of the evening. Guard yourself carefully against such false and deceitful thoughts that keep whispering: Wait awhile. In an hour or so I will pray. I must first finish this or that. Thinking such thoughts, we get away from prayer into business that will hold us and involve us till the prayer of the day comes to naught. . . .

Often enough, it happens that I so lose myself in the rich thoughts of one part or petition that I let the rest go. And when such rich, good thoughts come, one should let the other prayers go and give place to these thoughts. Listen to them in silence and on no account suppress them, for here the Holy Spirit is preaching to us, and a single word is worth more than a thousand of our own prayers. I have often learned more in one prayer than I could have obtained from much reading and pondering. . . .

Now a good, clever barber must have his thoughts, mind, and eyes concentrated upon the razor and the beard and not forget where he is in his stroke and shave. If he keeps talking or looking around or thinking of something else, he is like to cut a man's mouth and nose, or even his throat, so anything that is to be done well ought to occupy the whole man and all his faculties and members; as the saying goes: he who thinks of many things thinks of nothing and accomplishes no good. How much more must prayer possess the heart exclusively and completely if it is to be a good prayer!

. . . If I have time and opportunity after the Lord's Prayer, I do the same with the Ten Commandments, taking one part after another . . . and out of each part I make a garland of four twisted strands. That is, I take each first as a teaching, and reflect on what our Lord God so earnestly requires of me here. Secondly, I make of it a prayer of thanksgiving. Thirdly, a confession. Fourthly, a petition. . . .

But see to it that you do not undertake all of it or too much of it, lest your spirit become weary. Note too that a good prayer need not be long nor long-drawn-out, but rather should be frequent and ardent. It is sufficient if you can seize upon one part of even half of one part from which you can strike a spark in your heart. Well enough, the Spirit will and must grant this and will go on teaching in your heart if it is conformed to God's Word and cleared of foreign concerns and thoughts. Then, if you have time left over or are so inclined, you may do the same with the Creed and make of it a four-stranded garland.[2]

The fourth and final step of *lectio divina* is both the simplest and the hardest. It is nothing more than resting quietly in the sense

2. Luther, *Weimärer Ausgabe,* as translated in the *Minister's Prayer Book: An Order of Prayers and Readings,* ed. John W. Doberstein (Philadelphia: Fortress Press, 1986).

of God's presence that has been evoked and experienced in the preceding three steps. You let yourself just *be*, like the little child of Psalm 131, resting content in its mother's arms:

> El Shaddai, I want to avoid arrogance.
> I do not want to walk in ways too difficult for me,
> or try to understand things beyond my grasp.
> I calm myself now and sit quietly in Your embrace,
> like a weaned child at its mother's breast,
> my soul like a tranquil little one.
> With Your people, I hope in You, now and forevermore.[3]

Although this is the simplest step, it is just as important as the others, for it gives you time to truly enjoy the sense of the presence of God that is so often conveyed to us through the Word. This last step, called *contemplatio*, from which the English word "contemplation" is taken, is particularly hard for us in modern Western society, since we are so accustomed to rushing off to the next thing as soon as we have finished one thing. Our minds are so busy with a million concerns that it takes a while for us to get used to spending even a few minutes just gazing with love at God, like a baby gazing at its mother's face. Sometimes we are so tired that when we relax and try to contemplate, we fall asleep instead! Never mind. If we do, we probably need it, and there is nothing wrong with falling asleep in the arms of God, after all! The important thing is to try — to practice this as well as the other three steps of divine reading until they become natural, like breathing.

By regularly practicing *lectio divina* one or more times a week, we are building a foundation for our souls and our spiritual lives that will last forever. We are doing a good work that opens us up to the Holy Spirit's transforming grace in a most effective way. And, after a while, the habit of *lectio* spills over into our daily lives. We hear God speaking to us as we live day by day — perhaps in a sunrise or on a starlit night; perhaps in a hymn, a symphony,

---

3. From Marchiene Vroon Rienstra's *Swallow's Nest: A Feminine Reading of the Psalms* (Grand Rapids: William B. Eerdmans Publishing Co., 1992).

or even a popular song; perhaps in the words of a child, a friend, or a family member; perhaps in a painting or other work of art; perhaps in a dream or an idea. We become more and more sensitive to God's voice because we are learning to listen intensely for it in the words of Scripture. And the "spectacles of Scripture," to use John Calvin's telling image, in turn help us to see what God is saying in creation and history as well as in the particular events of our lives.

Our faith also deepens as we become used to the whole-hearted way of meditative prayer that is of the essence of *lectio divina*. We find ourselves responding in prayer to God as we go through each day and when we lie awake at night. Gradually, our thoughts become conversation with God. And we become better listeners and responders in our relationships with others, because we are listening and responding to God at ever-deeper levels. As we learn to rest in God's presence, we are able to trust more and more, and we discover how true is the promise we find in Isaiah: "In quietness and confidence shall be your strength; in returning and rest you shall be saved" (30:15).

Of course, all of this happens to the extent that we also actually *live* the Word we have read, pondered, prayed, and absorbed. We probably overestimate our ability to do this, just as we may overestimate it when we practice *lectio divina*, for we are often tempted to overload ourselves with too much of the Word. What we need to realize is that it often takes quite a while to integrate even a small amount of Scripture into our lives. And if we are going to do this with any real result, we need a lot of help and encouragement from others — and we also need them to hold us accountable.

A contemporary group of Christians that has grasped the importance of living the Word with accountability calls itself the Focolare movement, from the Italian word for hearth. An Italian woman named Chiara Lubich, along with a few of her women friends, began the Focolare movement in Italy during World War II. It is now a large, worldwide movement that is ecumenical and includes people of all ages. The heart of the group's spiritual practice is to make an intentional, concerted effort for a month at a time to live a "Word of Life," as they call it. Each month the group's international publication called "Living City" suggests a "Word of Life" and provides a meditation on its meaning.

For example, one month the "Word of Life" was John 17:22-23 (which is most important to them): "The glory that You have given Me I have given them, so that they may be one, as We are One, I in them and You in Me, that they may become completely one, so that the world may know that You have sent me and have loved them even as You have loved Me." All the Focolare folk — including the children — all over the world meditated upon the meaning of this passage and tried in every concrete way possible to live this Word of Life in their daily lives. They looked for ways to express loving unity with others in their families, their neighborhoods, and their workplaces. A child, for instance, might have looked for someone at school who seemed lonely and left out, and made a special effort to play with him or her as an expression of unity. An adult might have followed up a disagreement with someone by initiating a conversation in which the two of them could explore the common ground they may have had underneath the disagreement.

Each week the members of the Focolare movement meet in small local groups to pray, sing, and share their efforts to "live the Word."[4]

It is this kind of earnest integration of God's Word into their lives which makes them an attractive and wonderful witness, like the blazing Italian family hearth after which they are named. Through them, many whose hearts are cold and whose lives are forlorn are drawn to God's love, which warms and brightens their lives. It is an example which we would do well to follow, so that the Bread we eat is also the Bread we break and share with those who are hungering for the Word of Life.

The marvelous thing about all this is that *lectio divina* is universally accessible as a means of spiritual nourishment. Young and old, illiterate and well-educated, rich and poor — all kinds of people from all kinds of cultures can engage in divine reading. Unlike many of the Bible-study methods that are commonly used

4. From *Unity: Our Adventure: The Focolare Movement* (Brooklyn, N.Y.: New City Press, 1987).

in American churches, *lectio divina* does not depend on having Bibles, books, a curriculum, well-stocked libraries and bookstores, paper, copy machines and similar equipment, or the money it takes to secure these things. It doesn't even depend on the ability to read well. All that is needed is what the Holy Spirit promises and supplies — help with remembering what Jesus taught and guidance into further Truth.

How much in keeping it is with God's generous nature that the sustenance of the Word is offered to *all* who hunger and thirst! As Scripture says,

> Ho, everyone who thirsts, come to the waters; and you that have no money, come, buy and eat! Come, buy wine and milk without money and without price. Why do you spend your money for that which is not bread, and your labor for that which does not satisfy? Listen carefully to Me, and eat what is good, and delight yourselves in rich food! (Isa. 55:1, 2)

And it seems equally fitting that the Holy Spirit has throughout the ages inspired a way of receiving nourishment from Scripture that is so simple yet so profound, so readily available yet so transforming. Unlike the ways of using Scripture that are so shaped by Western, American, middle-and-upper-class assumptions and lifestyles, *lectio divina* has the flavor of Gospel authenticity, for it is Good News for absolutely anyone who hungers for the Word. And we can all practice it and teach it no matter where we go or who we are with — as long as the longing for the Truth is there!

Lectio divina is also Good News for the churches. In the first place, when ordained priests, ministers of the Word, elders, teachers, and so on are practicing divine reading faithfully, they have a profound and moving spiritual authority that cannot be attained any other way — not through any number of seminary courses or degrees, not through workshops or other training, not even by ordination. Though people can't always find words for it, they can sense it when those who are preaching and teaching the Word are personally hungry for it, when they themselves are ingesting it, praying it, and living it. Then the Word they preach and teach really nourishes those who are being fed. When a sermon or Sunday school lesson or other kind of Bible teaching is rooted in *lectio,* it rings true and edifies all who listen.

In addition, as church members practice divine reading, they become increasingly effective ministers of the Word in their homes, workplaces, and communities. Their lives are their pulpits, and they become prophets proclaiming God's Good News. There is little need for complicated evangelistic training programs and the like, for people who practice *lectio* naturally become effective and winsome witnesses of the Word that they have taken in and integrated into their hearts and lives.

Millions of Christians through many centuries have discovered that *lectio divina* is a satisfying way to eat the Bread on the Banqueting Table that God has prepared for all who will come to the Feast — Bread which is the "Staff of Life" for every one of God's people and for the church. It is the universal staple of the spiritual food that we all need. Therefore we offer this prayer, as we did at the beginning of this chapter:

Break Thou the Bread of Life, dear Lord, to me,
As Thou didst break the loaves beside the sea.
Beyond the sacred page I seek Thee, Lord.
My spirit yearns for Thee, O Living Word!

❋   ❋   ❋

The following are some specific spiritual exercises to help you further explore the material in this chapter and integrate it into your life:

1. Take between half an hour and an hour a few times during the week to try *lectio divina* in a couple of different ways. Follow the four steps outlined here, using a few variations of your choice, and record what you experience as you do.
2. Use *lectio divina* with another person or a small group, and notice how it differs from your practicing it alone. Record your experience and observations in your journal.

3. With another person or a small group, try choosing a "Word" to live for a week or a month, "Focolare style," and share your experiences. Reflect on these in your journal.
4. Make your own connections between the material in this chapter and one or more of the following passages: the story of Jesus' first temptation in the wilderness (Matt. 4:1-4), the feeding of the five thousand (John 6:1-15), and the discourse on the Bread of Life (John 6:22-59).

Books for Further Reflection

1. *Centering Prayer: Renewing an Ancient Christian Prayer Form* by M. Basil Pennington
   This Benedictine author describes a way to practice divine reading meditatively that is both practical and transformative. He places the practice in the context of a whole life centered in God.

2. *Space for God: The Study and Practice of Spirituality and Prayer* by Donald H. Postema
   Using art, especially works by Van Gogh, and a contemplative approach, the author explores how to meditatively listen for the Word of God in our lives. The book, which reflects the Reformed tradition from which Postema comes, includes numerous exercises.

3. *Unity: Our Adventure: The Focolare Movement* by New City Press
   This is the inspiring account of the history, vision, and life of the Focolare movement. The foremost emphasis of this account is living the Word, which is described in a way that is universally applicable.

CHAPTER 3

Fruitful Silence

No feast would be complete without an array of fruits. Their glorious colors and interesting shapes and textures, as well as their tastiness and nutritional value, make them a healthy and delightful part of our physical diet. Just so, the fruits of silence and solitude are part of the spiritual nourishment God provides for us at the Banqueting Table.

The Bible speaks often of the fruitfulness of God's land of promise and the fruitfulness of lives that are rooted in that promise. Psalm 1, for example, praises the person who meditates day and night upon God's Word. The Psalm says the person is like a tree planted by the waters that brings forth fruit in its season.

When I imagine such a person, and see in my mind's eye a tree planted by a river or lake, there is no noise in the picture. A profound silence prevails. It is a silence about which Scripture often speaks — often in connection with the wilderness. "Be still, and know that I am God," says the Word.

For many centuries, the wilderness has been a place of solitude in which people have met God and have wrestled with the shadows of darkness in the world and in their own souls and lives. In the process, they have been purified and transformed. In the vast silences of the desert, they have heard God's voice and call and have been given a new vision. They have been comforted, and they have received the gifts and energy to be powerfully effective partners with God for the fulfillment of God's desires and promises. This is so much the case that the terms "wilderness" and "desert" have become metaphors for spiritual testing and transformation.

The example of Moses comes immediately to mind. After a privileged childhood in Pharaoh's palace, he was forced to flee to the desert after his impetuous attempt to take matters into his own hands in response to the oppression of his people, the Israelites (Exod. 2:11-16). For many long years, Moses tended sheep in the wilderness. During those days of solitude, he had to face the shadows of his lack of dependence on God, his impetuosity, and his failure when he tried to help his own people.

Then he met God in a most unexpected way — in a blazing bush! Like so many after him, Moses had to confront his inadequate and mistaken ideas about God and face the awesome reality of God on the holy ground of God's own choosing. All his notions about himself, his abilities, his life, and God were shaken to the core. He was challenged with a vision of God's compassion for the chosen people and God's intent to deliver them from bondage. Out of the burning bush, God commissioned Moses to be God's spokesperson to Pharaoh, to demand freedom for Israel. For Moses, it meant taking a huge risk and facing a seemingly impossible task. At that point, God made Moses face the shadow of his fear and his feelings of inadequacy. In the end, Moses received the knowledge and the signs of God's powerful presence, as well as the promise of human help in the person of his brother Aaron to enable him to follow God's call (Exod. 3, 4).

Some time later, the whole nation of Israel followed Moses out of Egypt back into the desert. Through years of wilderness wandering they too, like Moses, were tested and purified. They had to face the slavish habits of being that still lurked in their hearts before they were fit to be the free people whom God was leading them to be. They had to learn to be responsible, to tell right from wrong, and to do right. They had to destroy their false images of God, both external and internal, and make the One True God an integral part of themselves and their society. They had to learn to move from grumbling against God to trusting in God, especially when the going got tough. They had to become aware of the reality of God's presence in their midst day and night, and they needed to learn to honor that presence in worship that spilled over into their everyday lives.

A long time later, a prophet who would be ranked with Moses as among the greatest of Israel's leaders also went into the desert. His name was Elijah, and he, like Moses, fled into the desert because his life was threatened (1 Kings 19). There, in spite of his great triumph over the prophets of Baal at Mount Carmel, Elijah was forced to face the shadows of his failure to win God's people back to covenant faithfulness, as well as his own despair and sense of abandonment. His inner darkness was so great that he simply didn't wish to live anymore.

It was when he had reached this low point in the desert that Elijah experienced the tender care and mercy of God. The angel of God's presence provided food for his journey, and with it the extraordinary strength he needed to come to Horeb — the "Mount of God" — the same place where Moses, and then Israel, had experienced life-changing epiphanies of God's presence and reality. In a cave — an archetypal metaphor for going "inward" — Elijah heard God's voice and experienced God's presence in a way that challenged all his previous experience. At Mount Carmel, God had been manifest in the storm and fire from heaven. But now it was in the "still, small voice" or "sheer silence" (19:12, NRSV) that Elijah experienced and heard God. In that purifying encounter in the solitude and silence of the wilderness, Elijah was renewed. He was given a new commission and call, and also given the courage and ability to fulfill it.

Moses, Israel, and Elijah all anticipated the wilderness experience of Jesus, in whom all their prophecy and work came to fulfillment. The Gospels tell us that it was the Holy Spirit who "drove" Christ into the wilderness to be tempted — to face the Shadow behind all shadows of human evil. Before Jesus could enter into his public ministry, he too needed to confront the evil possibilities of the human nature that he had assumed. In the silence and solitude of the desert, Jesus had to wrestle with his identity, his powers, and his mission and how he would accomplish it.

His Adversary tried to get him to prove that he was God's beloved and chosen — as if God's Word were not enough proof! (Matt. 4; Luke 4). Christ faced the temptations common to human beings: his Adversary tempted him to exploit nature for self-centered ends, to wield political power over people, and to take self-aggrandizing risks. Christ wrestled with each of these temptations in a way unique to his own person and calling. And at the end of — perhaps even during — the fasting and the struggle, he was strengthened by the angels of God's Spirit and the presence of wild animals (Mark 1:12-13). Rooted and grounded in God's Word, filled with the Holy Spirit and wisdom of God, and imbued with the power of God's presence, Jesus returned to Galilee and began his teaching and healing ministry (Luke 4:14-15).

Many times during his ministry, Jesus would retire to the wilderness to be alone with God, and sometimes he would take his disciples along. Remarkable things would often happen around these times or during them — perhaps the most remarkable being the Transfiguration. At that point the disciples saw Jesus as he really was in all his glory. The Gospel of Luke in particular makes a point of portraying these "wilderness times" as essential to Jesus' life and ministry, and to that of the disciples.

In the days of the early church, and especially after the "fall" of the church as a result of the Constantinian change, Christians went into the wilderness to be alone with God. Always it was because they knew they needed the purification of meeting God in the silence and solitude that the desert provided, and the absolute sense of dependence on God that was part of the experience. When Christianity became the official religion of the Roman Empire and the church became corrupt, these men and women found it necessary to flee into the wilderness, because they knew they were too weak to resist the soul-destroying influences of the society in which they lived. They found that they could not be faithful to the Gospel except by dwelling, at least for a significant time, in the wilderness, either alone or in community.

They discovered that they had to saturate their minds and hearts with the Gospels, the Psalms, and other Scriptures. They had to wrestle with the "demons" that dwelt in their souls — some of them demons that afflicted the whole culture as well: the demons of greed, lust, oppression, deceit, and the like. And they had to learn to become so conscious of the presence of God that they were able to move along with the breath of the Holy Spirit rather

32

than the winds of the age. The whole monastic movement of the church is rooted in their early experiences of purification, prayer, and the presence of God.

At its best, the presence of hermits and contemplative monastic communities has borne witness throughout the centuries to the need for sacred silence and solitude for spiritual health. It seems that the Holy Spirit has never stopped luring the people of God into the desert (Hos. 2:14-23) and speaking tenderly to them, restoring them to faithfulness and empowering them to witness to the corrupt generations of which they were a part.

That is still true today. We, no less than our ancestors in faith, need to follow the example of our Lord and make time for solitude and silence in our own lives. For we too are called by the Holy Spirit to encounter the shadows of evil in our own souls and in our society. We need to wrestle with the darkness within and without, free from the constant distractions of a busy life. We need to encounter the mysterious presence and reality of God and let it shatter all our false images and misconceptions, for there is not one of us who does not harbor idols, false images of God, in mind and heart.

Like Jesus, we are called to claim our identity as God's baptized and beloved daughters and sons. In order to do this, we must internalize God's incredible mercy and grace toward us. And we need to hear and accept God's unique vision and call for our lives and discern the gifts and powers that God has given to us (in spite of our fears and because of our inadequacies) to enable ourselves to be true to our God-given visions and vocations. Elizabeth O'Connor, in her book entitled *Eighth Day of Creation*, has this to say about it:

> We ask to know the will of God without guessing that God's will is written into our very beings. We perceive that will when we discern our gifts. Our obedience and surrender to God are, in large part, our obedience and surrender to our gifts. . . . When we deny our gifts, we blaspheme against the Holy Spirit, whose action is to call forth gifts. In every person is the creation story. Since the first day of our beginning, the Spirit has brooded over the formless, dark void of our lives, calling us into existence

33

through our gifts until they are developed. And that same Spirit gives us the responsibility of investing them with God in the continuing creation of the world. Our gifts are the signs of our commissioning, the conveyors of our human-divine love, the receptacles of our own transforming, creative power.[1]

It is hard, if not impossible, to receive God's transforming power, to share God's perspective on our lives and our society, and to experience God's incredible mercy and unconditional love if we don't take time away from the demands of our daily routines — just as one cannot get the perspective a mountaintop gives without going there! The wilderness of silence and solitude is a place for the challenge and transformation we need if we are to be effective partners with God in God's redemptive purposes.

A wise Christian woman once admonished me about the importance of all this by saying, "Either draw apart or fall apart!" A desert father of long ago said that the greatest enemies of the spiritual life are hurry, crowds, and noise. We who live in the midst of these things need to recognize the wisdom of occasional flight into the wilderness of silence and solitude to be alone with God. We will be conformed to the status quo of this world if we do not remove ourselves from it to give God a chance to renew our minds, and to give ourselves a chance to know God's good and perfect will for the world and for us (cf. Rom. 12:1-2).

We are probably thinking of ourselves more highly than we ought to if we imagine that we are strong enough to resist the pressures of the culture in which we are constantly immersed. And we are falling even shorter of the glory of God than we otherwise would if we do not take the time to ponder upon our experience and our selves, and sort through what other people think, what we think, and what God thinks, so that we can move from confusion to clarity on the vital issues of our lives. In short, if we are to become all that God meant us to be, there is no substitute for sacred silence and solitude, and holy leisure.

It is important to stress this need because there are a great

---

1. O'Connor, *Eighth Day of Creation: Discovering Your Gifts and Using Them* (Waco, Tex.: Word Books, 1971), pp. 15, 17.

many difficulties with, objections to, misunderstandings of, and resistance to this kind of retreat, both in us and in our society. If that were not so, there would be no need to remind ourselves of the importance of silence and solitude.

One of the foremost objections comes out of the activist mentality, which includes the belief that one's worth as a Christian is measured by how much one is "doing for the Lord." This belief leaves little room and no comfort for those who, as Milton wrote in his blindness, can only "stand and wait." It does not allow for the holiness of being, resting in God's Being, and the value of simply existing as one of God's beloved creatures. It insists that one must constantly be at work.

Garrison Keillor has poked gentle fun of this attitude in "The Prairie Home Companion," his NPR radio show, by calling the local Catholic church in his little Minnesota town "Our Lady of Perpetual Responsibility." Of course, Protestants are no strangers to this attitude! In fact, the Protestant Reformation not only threw out the life of the hermit and the monastic as unsuitable for the servants of God, but also posited the "Protestant work ethic" in its place, and pushed the significance of contemplation and holy leisure to the outer edges of the Christian life. We are all the worse for it.

Besides the objections of the activist mentality and the work ethic, there is a closely related objection to taking ample time for silence and solitude: that it is irresponsible and "other-worldly" — a pious flight from real life into the never-never land of selfish spirituality. Of course, anyone who has actually gone into the wilderness of silence and solitude can testify that it is anything but a flight from real life. In fact, it is often the case that Christians try to escape from knowing and dealing with what is really going on in their hearts and lives and the society around them by being busy. Busyness has, in fact, become an addiction and a point of pride. Who dares admit to not being busy? To do so might be to admit that one is unimportant!

This brings to mind one of the greatest difficulties people have in taking the time they need for the "wilderness" experience. That difficulty is fear — fear of the spiritual depths, fear of what one might find in one's heart, fear of encounter with God as God

Is, fear of what one might be asked to do or how one might be challenged to change. It is a fear that is very deep-rooted in our psyches; it goes all the way back to the Fall and to the fear of God that Adam and Eve expressed when they hid in the bushes from God's presence. We are all afflicted with this fear of God, of the spiritual depths, and of change. Until we confront it, we will find a million reasons not to try fruitful silence. After all, our egos are often heavily invested in the status quo.

Unfortunately, experience has shown (and certain television evangelists are a prime example) that work for God which is not deeply rooted in the soil of meditation and prayer (Psalm 1) will not bear much fruit for the reign of God; in fact, it will often be full of egotism, because it involves little self-knowledge and little genuine communion with God. So, if we want to be genuinely fruitful for God, we need to take time to abide in the Vine.

Once we decide to try to do this, we often find that making the time for silence and solitude doesn't seem practical. How can one make time in the face of so many commitments? What place can one go that is safe and available and not hard to get to? And where can one find guidance and support for spending time alone with God? These are genuine issues, and yet they are not impossible to resolve. Underlying them is the reality of our "enmeshment" in the affairs of this life. It often takes a serious and sudden accident or illness or natural disaster to remind us of what is always true — that our lives are uncertain at best, and that all the things we think are so important really are not. Only a basic few are: life, love, loved ones.

The kind of "holy detachment" that is a primary virtue of the Christian life is the opposite of this "enmeshment" that often pulls us in many different directions and prevents our living with true integrity. To be detached in a holy way from our egos, our plans, our work, and even our loved ones and commitments is to be attached so strongly to God that we hold all of God's gifts to us lightly, willing to let them go when God calls. This is certainly what Jesus was talking about when he said that we cannot be his disciples if we do not "hate [meaning "separate ourselves from"] father and mother, wife and children, brothers and sisters, yes, and even life itself" (Luke 14:25-33).

If we cannot leave whatever and whoever we need to for a short time to be alone with God, how can we be ready to leave them for a longer time, or forever, if Christ calls? Can we be disciples of Christ if we are not willing to extricate ourselves for a while (usually a much shorter while than the first disciples did) in order to "company with Christ" or to let the Holy Spirit lead or drive us into the wilderness? There is great wisdom in the old proverb "Where there's a will, there's a way." Elizabeth O'Connor puts it like this:

> When you feel very strongly about something, do you consider it difficult to put into action? It is only when you don't vitally feel the truth of something that you say it is difficult to put into action. You don't love it. That which you love you do with ardour, there is joy in it, and then what society or loved ones may say does not matter. But if you are not deeply convinced, if you do not feel free and happy in doing what you think is right, surely your interest in it is false, unreal; therefore it becomes mountainous and you say it is difficult to put into action. In doing what you love to do there will, of course, be difficulties, but that won't matter to you. It is part of life.[2]

That is the heart of it. If you are honest, the call to the wilderness will reveal to you what your real reasons are for avoiding sacred silence and holy solitude. And that in turn will give you great opportunity for repentance and spiritual growth. Then, if you are willing to take the risk and make the effort, if you love God enough to want time alone with God, just as you do with other persons whom you love, then you will find a way. And if you look to God and pray earnestly for help in finding a way, you will find that it will be provided by the God who lures you into the wilderness and delights in your undivided attention! Already, there is much in place to help you.

First, there is the gift of many retreat centers — places to which you can go for silence and solitude. They have an atmosphere that allows for both; and often there are prayerful and experienced

2. O'Connor, *Eighth Day of Creation*, p. 97.

spiritual guides who will give you the support you need, especially at first. The fees of these centers are very reasonable; some even charge nothing, although they appreciate donations. They are located in every part of this country, and in other countries as well.

Second, there are people, maybe only one or two, whom you can ask to encourage and support you, and to whom you can hold yourself accountable for taking the necessary time. Their support and prayer can make a big difference. It may even be that the community of faith to which you belong would help you in this way. It's definitely worth a try.

You might find unexpected help at home too. Some people I know have created a little "prayer corner" or room for themselves and established the rule that when anyone is praying in this sacred space, he or she is not to be disturbed. Believe it or not, children learn to respect this (the younger they are, the shorter the time you spend in the corner needs to be, of course) and even to claim time in it for themselves. The phone can always be turned off, and other intrusions can be eliminated for an hour or even a day on a regular basis.

Third, there is the wonderful device of the calendar. I have found that if I simply put a date on my calendar each month for "wilderness time" (usually 24 hours), do this for several months or even a year in advance, and make reservations at the places where I wish to go, I am usually able to keep the commitment. When I am asked — inevitably — to do this or that on that date, my response is simple: "Oh, I'm sorry, but I already have an important commitment on my calendar." And that's all I need to say. In our society the calendar is almost a little god. But you can press it into holy service if you are so minded!

Fourth, there are many resources, found in the books suggested below and in the bibliography, that provide guidance for entering into silence. The important thing is to be willing to let go of your pre-set agendas for your time apart and let the Holy Spirit guide you. Your own deepest needs will surface if you let them, and you will be able to find what it is that God wants to do with, in, and for you. Don't try to squeeze yourself into anyone else's agenda! And don't let the advice found in books or given by someone else be a substitute for discerning your own authentic direction during your time of silence. Consult rather than conform to what comes from outside the sanctuary of your heart, where the Holy Spirit dwells.

With this in mind, you might try some of the following suggestions to see how they help you enter into silence.

The first suggestion is — or seems like — a simple one. Try entering into silence by using your senses. This is a great way to quiet the flurry of thoughts and feelings that may be keeping you from experiencing inner silence. Sit quietly, free of interruption, and "tune in" to what you are hearing, feeling, smelling, seeing. Listen for wisdom and inspiration. Sometimes you'll become aware of some physical discomfort that could have an important message for you about how you're living. Sometimes the things you have set up in a prayer corner or room, or what you see if you're outdoors — say, in your backyard or a nearby park — will speak to you in a spiritual way.

One day, for example, as I was sitting quietly in my prayer corner, I became acutely aware of the pain in my back and the tension in my shoulders. "What are you trying to tell me?" I asked my body in a silent but playful way. "That you are overloaded" came the reply in the form of words that welled up from somewhere in me. They hit home because it was true. I was overloaded, and I had been trying to ignore this fact. But my body spoke the truth when I was quiet enough to listen to it. After all, if God could speak to Balaam through his ass, should I be surprised if I get a message from God through my body?

On another occasion, I was at Morning Star, a favorite retreat center of mine, and was sitting by the stream that runs near the cabin where I stay. As I sat there in silence, a dragonfly came and perched on my bare knee! It just sat there for the longest time, and I marveled at its trust and its delicate beauty. I sat very still, not wanting to scare it. By the time it flew off, I was thinking about perching in God's presence with trust, like the dragonfly. It was a wonderful revelation.

Another way to enter into silence is to take ten to twenty minutes and sit quietly, repeating a word that makes you feel the presence of God: perhaps the word "love" or "joy" or "holy," or one of God's names. It helps to close your eyes and remember that God's Holy Spirit dwells within you. Or to think of yourself as a little child resting in God's arms as you repeat your sacred word. Whenever you find that your mind is wandering, just call it back into God's presence with your word, and keep doing this until the time you have decided upon is up. (Some people use a timer with a soft chime or a watch alarm.) The busyness of your mind, the noise of inner chatter, is calmed by this method, and though it's hard to maintain inner silence for very long, it does become easier as you practice this form of silence, which is called centering prayer.

Another way to do something very similar is to choose a short prayer of a few words that includes a name for God and a brief request that expresses your deepest need at this point in your life. This becomes your "breath prayer," and you repeat it for ten or more minutes, always returning to it when your mind wanders. Some examples of breath prayers include "Holy Spirit, make me whole," "Jesus Christ, have mercy on me," and "Dear Lord, fill me with your Love." It helps to stick with one for a month or so, and take your breath prayer with you into your day. Use it as often as you can as a way of entering into inner silence and the sense of God's presence, not only when you are alone with God but as you go about living your day. If you wake during the night, the breath prayer is a wonderful way to deal creatively with insomnia. It is also helpful when you're tired and sick and feel too weak to pray with many words. Young and old and in between — all ages and kinds of people have found this a simple and wonderful way to pray silently.

I believe that the Holy Spirit inspires these prayers, and that they are answered. That is my experience, at least. And when one prayer is answered, a new one is given. Once, for example, I was led to use "Dear God, help me listen" as my breath prayer. After several months, I became aware that I had gotten much better at listening to other people as well as to God. I was ready for the next breath prayer the Holy Spirit (whose name in Hebrew and Greek means "breath"!) would give me.

A third and more active way to enter into silence is to try walking meditation. Take a slow walk, timing your steps with your inhaling and exhaling, and then add to your walk a breath prayer, or one of God's names, or "Alleluia," or whatever else suits you. Try to have a gentle, relaxed half-smile on your face, and perhaps imagine beautiful flowers springing up behind you. Again, when you catch your mind wandering, getting noisy and busy, just recall it with your breath and the word or words you are saying, and continue walking in silence.

This approach can be extended by engaging in some simple, grounding activities like knitting, gardening, washing dishes, and folding clothes in a slow, serene way. Use your eyes and nose and hands and ears to focus on what you're doing, and enjoy the simple pleasure of the click of knitting needles, the smell and feel of earth and plants, the warmth of dishwater, the color and texture of clothes. Enter silently and fully into the present moment and the gift that it is. God comes to us in humble ways through creation — which is, after all, God's handiwork, and therefore a means of communing with God. A beautiful line from a song in the film *Brother Sun, Sister Moon* puts it this way: "If you want to live life free, take your time, go slowly; do few things, and do them well; simple joys are holy."

❀　　　❀　　　❀

When we spend time communing with God in silence in all these ways we have been exploring, we find ourselves bearing more and more of the fruit of the Holy Spirit. Our lives become filled with joy, which is not the absence of pain but rather the experience of the presence of God. We become more peaceful and centered. Gradually, our hearts become quiet sanctuaries in which we commune with God even in the midst of much activity. We become more deeply connected to our true selves — the Christ-like image of God that the Holy Spirit is restoring within us. We connect more strongly to creation and to others in a growing spirit of appreciation and love. We begin to know by experience what it means to live and move and have our being in God, who is above all, and through all, and in all.

As we allow the Holy Spirit to knit together the broken parts of our lives and make us more whole, we live with greater integrity. We have a new awareness of our selves, both our shadows and our gifts, and with it, we have more humility and humor! We become easier to live with and gentler with ourselves and others. We have a clearer vision for our lives and for the world, based on God's vision.

Amazingly, we find that we have more energy and more time.

41

For time is strangely like elastic — it stretches and contracts. Clocks and calendars are actually human structures that are, at least in part, illusions. We find that we are able to do what is really important. And we can let go of all the unimportant things that serve only to burden us unnecessarily. We become aware of more of our gifts and become empowered to use them as we respond to God's call, which we have heard in the still places of our lives. All this, and much more, is the fruit of sacred silence and holy solitude.

There is an ancient prayer to the Holy Spirit that is among the best prayers for entering into the silence and solitude of which we have been speaking. It reveals most eloquently what God longs to give us when we are still and ready to receive it:

> Holy Spirit, send from heaven a spark of Your radiant Heart.
> Mother of the poor, bestowing gifts on those in need,
> Come, Source of Life, within our hearts.
> Deepest Source of consolation dwelling in our souls,
> You give pilgrims their repose.
> To the toiling You give rest.
> You cool the burning heat and comfort those in tears.
> O most joyful like a Bride,
> fill the secret hearts of those who trust in You.
> Without the Presence of Your Godhead,
> nothing lies in us, nothing free from harm.
>
> Wash what is soiled,
> water what is dry,
> heal what is wounded.
> Bend what is rigid,
> warm what is cold,
> find what is lost.
>
> Grant to those who believe and trust in You
> the sacred gifts and fruits of Your Presence.
> Grant us the reward of Your work in us.
> Consummate our life in peace.
> Grant us joy forever.
> Amen. Alleluia!

❋   ❋   ❋

Here are some specific spiritual exercises to help you further explore the material in this chapter and integrate it into your life:

1. In your journal, reflect on your experience of solitude and silence thus far in your life.
2. List all the difficulties you have with taking the time to "go into the wilderness." Try to discern, in prayer, what might be at their root. Choosing one or more forms of expression — words, music, movement, modeling clay, drawing, or painting — describe whatever it is, and dialogue with it.
3. Offer all the difficulties and their root cause(s) to God by writing them down on a piece of paper and then burning or burying them as a way of letting them go that gets beyond your head and into your heart.
4. Try the ancient Christian practice of "Holy Vigil." This is one way to do it:

    If you wake up during the night, get up and spend some time in silence with God. Try just being, or offer a centering prayer. Or try any of the other possibilities discussed in this chapter.

    If you don't wake up during the night, or can't stay awake more than a few minutes when you do, get up an hour early or stay up an hour late just once during the week to honor Jesus' command to "watch and pray."
5. Take out your calendar and mark off at least one day during the next three months for your own "wilderness time." Make reservations at a retreat center, hold yourself accountable to somebody who will support and pray for your intention, and then "just do it"!

    Feel free to take your calendar and for the next year mark off a day a month for your pursuit of solitude. If you try it, you just might find that silence is fruitful — and delicious!

Books for Further Reference

1. *Poustinia* by Catherine Doherty
   This little classic by a remarkable Russian-American woman of this generation entices us into silent communion with God in a way that is full of common sense and adapted to life in North America.

2. *The Breath of Life: A Simple Way to Pray* by Ron DelBene et al.
   This book provides a foundational understanding of "breath prayer" and explains how it can help one live contemplatively and learn to pray in inner silence. Del Bene draws heavily on the classic teachings on prayer and silence, especially in the Orthodox tradition, but he makes them contemporary and practical.

3. *Out of Solitude* by Henri J. Nouwen
   This wonderful little book by a beloved author has become a classic statement on the spiritual life and on the benefits of solitude and silence for all Christians.

4. *Open Mind, Open Heart: The Contemplative Dimension of the Gospel* by Thomas Keating
   In this book Keating gives guidance for praying in silence and for learning how to pray and live contemplatively. He discusses the beliefs and attitudes that undergird this kind of prayer and suggests some very helpful techniques for practicing it. He speaks eloquently of the transforming power of such prayer.

5. *A Guide to Monastic Guest Houses* by J. Robert Beagle
   This is one of several guidebooks to retreat centers that are available from bookstores and Hugen Press. In addition, the Catholic magazines *Praying* and *National Catholic Reporter,* which are available from many local Catholic churches and libraries, regularly carry advertisements for retreat centers.

CHAPTER 4

Physical Spirituality

If the notion of physical spirituality jars us, it is because we are inheritors of a Western European tradition that has torn asunder what God has always intended to be united — that is, the physical and the spiritual, the body and the soul. The Bible clearly teaches that God made our bodies and this physical world and loves them as much as the invisible spiritual part of us and of creation. God does not offer soul food to us as disembodied creatures! Spirituality and sensuousness are not opposites but partners in God's provision for our spiritual health. In fact, our souls are nourished at the Feast through our senses.

Unfortunately, we Western Christians, especially those of us from the Protestant tradition, have often not understood the physical side of being spiritual. It is difficult for us to think of our bodies, our senses, and the material world as means of communion with God and therefore as profoundly "spiritual." We are used to a way of thinking that separates body and soul, the physical and the spiritual, heaven and earth.

For example, in one of the most influential modern theological "schools," based on Karl Barth's theology, God is completely transcendent and is seen as the "totally Other." Most people's idea of the "kingdom of heaven" or the "kingdom of God" is that it is a place way above and beyond us somewhere. The spiritual is considered to be closely connected to the heavenly and to God and is therefore often thought of as "otherworldly." It has little to do with the earth, the flesh, or our ordinary, very physical lives.

Many of us Christians today are not so different from our medieval ancestors in faith, who closely linked the world, the flesh, and the devil. Sadly, we separate prayer and politics, piety and justice, the inward journey and the outward journey. In doing so, we reveal the extent to which (often unconsciously) we are conformed to this secular age, which has pushed God to the parameters of life and tried to limit truth to what human reason and science determine.

This secular mind-set privatizes prayer and faith and rules it out of the arena of public learning, discourse, and action. Christians who fail to make the connection between beliefs and business, prayer and politics, and the spiritual and the physical are victims of an unholy dichotomy. They are also prevented from enjoying the delicious milk and honey of *sens*ible spiritual food that God is constantly providing for us all at the Banqueting Table.

Of course, there are some powerful historical reasons for this state of affairs that are helpful to examine and understand. We are inheritors of the Greek philosophical tradition, which profoundly shaped Christian theology from its earliest days. Greek thought, unlike Hebrew thought, considered God to be the "Unmoved Mover" and "First Cause" who was perfect in part by virtue of the fact that "he" was beyond all passion or any kind of connection to the material. The human spirit was considered to be imprisoned in the body, and "salvation" was in good part the ability to be free of and "beyond" the physical.

The two extremes of severe asceticism and physical self-indulgence were practiced by many religious sects influenced by this kind of thinking. Ascetics considered control, discipline, and even punishment of the body to be the only way to free the spirit from its demands. Those who indulged themselves in orgies of eating, drinking, sex, and the like believed that since the body was not holy, it didn't matter what one did with it. Needless to say, the ascetic approach had by far the greatest influence among early Christians, though there are plenty of passages in the Epistles which indicate that the other extreme was a real and present danger in the churches of that time.

By contrast, Hebrew thought was founded on the goodness of the physical creation and considered human beings primarily from a physical point of view. Even the spirit was physical — that is, it was breath, quite literally — and the soul was a shadowy, indefinable something that went to the shadowland of Sheol at death. There was no concept, as in Greek thought, of human immortality and the immortal soul. Moreover, God was considered to be passionate and compassionate and constantly involved in the created world, as the historical books of the Old Testament amply testify. Creation, the body, and the senses were all portrayed — especially in the Psalms — as involved in the worship of God and in communion with God. The just and loving treatment of people, including concern for their physical well-being, was considered an essential aspect of worshiping and serving God, particularly according to the prophets. All Hebrew Scriptures testify to this faith stance, and it is due to their influence in the early church that the early church did not go any further than it did in accepting the strain of Greek philosophical thought which considered the spiritual good and the material evil.

In the Eastern churches, which came to be called Orthodox, a profound sacramental doctrine of the Incarnation and the Resurrection, with all that both imply about the holiness of the body and matter, prevented the degree of dichotomy between the physical and the spiritual that has plagued the Western churches, both Catholic and Protestant. That dichotomy is evidenced in the strong iconoclastic streak that prevailed in parts of the Catholic tradition and in almost all of Protestant Christianity, resulting in a contempt for the body and for the physical, a contempt that is seen in many tragic chapters in church history.

The Crusades and the sacking of Constantinople; the destruction of priceless religious art in the cathedrals by leaders of the Reformation, especially Cromwell and his troops in England; the severe and pathological ascetic practices in some of the monasteries; the persecution and burning of many thousands of women as witches; and, in more recent times, the assault on the earth — all of these, and more, are expressions of the false dichotomy between body and spirit, mind and matter, and a negative attitude toward the physical.

Until recently, much of the advice given by the religious leaders who have written "spiritual books" has been unfriendly to the body and the senses, because it has been influenced by this false dichotomy. For example, in one of the great classics of the spiritual life, *The Spiritual Exercises* of St. Ignatius, Ignatius says, "In meditation on subject matter that is not visible . . . the mental image will consist of imagining, and considering my soul imprisoned in its corruptible body, and my entire being in this vale of tears as an exile among brute beasts."

Protestant hymnody sometimes reflects the same attitude toward the body and the senses — that is, that they are impediments to the spiritual life. For instance, the last verse of the well-known hymn "Dear Lord and Father of Mankind" says this: "Breathe through the heats of our desire Thy coolness and Thy balm; let sense be dumb, let flesh retire."

To be honest, I must admit that there are passages in Scripture which seem to give "aid and comfort" to the body/soul dichotomy. Several examples are found in the letters of Paul. One such passage seems to take a negative view of the body: "Athletes exercise self-control in all things; they do it to receive a perishable wreath, but we an imperishable one. So I do not run aimlessly, nor do I box as though beating the air; but I punish my body and enslave it, so that after proclaiming to others I myself should not be disqualified" (1 Cor. 9:25-27). Another passage opposes flesh and Spirit: "Live by the Spirit, I say, and do not gratify the desires of the flesh. For what the flesh desires is opposed to the Spirit, and what the Spirit desires is opposed to the flesh; for these are opposed to each other, to prevent you from doing what you want" (Gal. 5:16-17).

Peter and John say similar things in their epistles. "Beloved," says Peter, "I urge you as aliens and exiles to abstain from the desires of the flesh that wage war against the soul" (1 Pet. 2:11). "Do not love the world or the things in the world," John admonishes. "The love of the Father is not in those who love the world; for all that is in the world — the desire of the flesh, the desire of the eyes, the pride in riches — comes not from the Father but from the world" (1 John 2:15-16).

Christians of every generation import meanings into Scripture

48

as they interpret it, for we are all children of our age. It is easy to see why Christians who were living in a world powerfully influenced by Greek philosophy came to interpret passages such as these as posing a dichotomy between the physical and the spiritual, and strongly favoring the spiritual over against the physical.

Fortunately, we have the advantage of many intervening centuries, and we are able to detect how Greek thought led to misinterpretation of these texts. No doubt we have our own blind spots in our generation and cannot see ways in which the cultural assumptions we have absorbed influence how we interpret Scripture. But at least today there is a move away from the dichotomy. The teaching of the creation account, which stresses the goodness of the physical creation and our whole beings, body and soul, as created by God, is being recovered as a foundational belief. Contemporary Christian thinkers are realizing the tragic results of the body/soul dichotomy that has plagued so much of Western Christianity. More and more Christians of every kind are beginning to see the importance of what is called a "sacramental" spirituality, which sees all life as holy, and the ordinary and the physical, including our bodies, as a means of communion with God.

In the work of some current writers, the pendulum seems to be swinging the other way, so much so that there is no longer any clear distinction made between the body and the spirit or soul. The unity of the two is stressed so greatly that the differences are ignored. This viewpoint creates problems of its own for faith and life. For one thing, it ignores our experience. It is true that our bodies and our physical environment greatly affect our spirits, and vice versa, but experience teaches us that our bodies and souls are distinct. There are many people, for example, who find that their "inner selves" or "spirits" do not seem to be the same age as their bodies! And there are those whose spirits seem to be able to experience joy and peace even when their bodies are suffering. Of course, most Christians also share the belief that when their bodies die, their spirits live on in heaven with God. Until the final resurrection of the dead, there is a separation of body and spirit. The many stories of "after-death" experiences that have surfaced in the past several years seem to support the idea that we have a "spiritual body" which can and does live independently of the physical body.

COME TO THE FEAST

Although it is not accurate to interpret scriptural passages such as those I cited earlier as opposing the spirit to the body, it is important to see that Scripture, especially the New Testament, does treat body and spirit as closely related but not identical. The famous chapter on the resurrection of the body, 1 Corinthians 15, is a case in point.

In addition, in the passages in which they occur, the terms for "flesh," "body," and "world" have far more sophisticated meanings than a simplistic dualistic interpretation allows for. A close study reveals that these words refer as much to "invisible" as to visible or physical aspects of life. Paul, Peter, and John all associate malice, envy, quarreling, lying, greed, injustice, and the like with the body, the flesh, and the world. These words might better be understood as referring to human nature and the structures of society insofar as they are separate from and opposed to God and God's love and justice.

The important thing is to see scriptural references to the flesh, the body, the spirit, the world, and so on in the context of the entire Bible and its great themes of Creation, the Fall, Redemption and Salvation, and the promise of the New Creation. When they are seen in this framework, it is clear that the original goodness of creation and of human beings includes their physicality. From the beginning, God intended for all human beings to commune with Godself through and with the senses. Creation was meant to be transparent to the presence of its Creator, so that all of life — eating, sleeping, making love, playing, walking, working, creating, tending creation, delighting in God's creatures — would be a means of communion between people and God.

Isn't it fascinating that the very first thing that happened after Adam and Eve became alienated from God through their act of distrust and defiance is that they became self-conscious and ashamed, and made loincloths out of leaves to hide themselves? The first symptom of their sin was shameful alienation from their own bodies! And after that came the further alienation from and negative experience of the physical: in the pain that would accompany childbirth for women; in the blaming of and domination of women by men; and in humankind's adversarial, struggle-ridden relationship with the earth — all leading to death.

50

Before the Fall, man and woman experienced life, including the physical aspects of it, as delightful and good, as spiritual communion with God. They were the high priests of creation, receiving the good gifts of life in all their fullness and materiality and offering them back to God in thanksgiving and praise. After the Fall, the physical and relational became an experience of evil as well as good for them. Creation became opaque — that is, it was no longer transparent to the presence of God. Instead, the experience of the presence of God became elusive and problematic. The hearts of human beings were changed, and they constantly strayed from God's presence and doubted divine love. No longer did they see God in all; no longer did they enjoy God's presence in each ordinary moment. Instead, they fled into the bushes of concealment and alienation. We know from personal experience what all of this is like, because each of us lives the Fall in our own lives.

But God never left us human beings in our own self-made misery. In due course, after centuries of preparing a people, God became flesh in Jesus Christ. The Incarnation reunited alienated spirit and flesh, God and humans, heaven and earth, the spiritual and the material, in the most profound and far-reaching way possible. All matter, all creation, was redeemed along with us humans.

Because the Word has become flesh, all flesh — every atom — is holy. Because Christ entered time, every moment of every day has been redeemed. The gap between God and human beings was closed by Jesus Christ's birth, life, and death. The suffering of Christ, into which all human suffering is taken up, unites even our negative experience of the body in pain with Christ's pain and makes it holy. When we see our suffering in this way and offer it to Christ, it becomes redemptive in mysterious ways that transcend reasoning but are very real nevertheless.

The bodily resurrection from the dead that the Gospels so clearly attest to, and that Paul so vigorously defends in 1 Corinthians 15, completes the foundation laid by Christ's incarnation for a Christian reverence for the body, which Paul also calls "the temple of the Holy Spirit." The Bible says that Christ actually dwells *in* us, and Jesus tells us in Matthew 25, as well as in other

51

places, that we will be judged by how we treat others physically — especially "the least." Do we offer a drink, a meal, a garment? Do we welcome the homeless into our house? Visit the sick and the imprisoned? Receive a little child? Then we have done these things for him!

As if all this were not enough to convince us of the physical aspect of being spiritual, we are promised a new heaven and a new earth — not just a new heaven. The whole creation is groaning now under the burden of human sin accumulated through many centuries. But it is also being redeemed and renewed, as are we, by the power of the Holy Spirit. Our future is one in which Jerusalem will come down from heaven, and the heavenly city will be united with the earth. In the New Creation that is coming, the split between our bodies and our spirits will be healed, as it was in Jesus' resurrected body. His body is the "firstfruit"; our bodies shall be like his glorious one.

No wonder God has poured out the milk and honey of sensuous delight at the Banqueting Table. We are invited to "taste and see that God is good"! And we are invited to do that with our bodies through all our senses. Creation has been restored for us as a gift that is once more transparent to the presence of God. In it and through it, we can commune with God and celebrate life! We have been placed with Christ at God's right hand (Eph. 2:4-10) in a "heavenly place" that is here and now; and in this place or state of being, we have "fullness of joy" and "pleasures forevermore" (Ps. 16). Those pleasures are physical as well as spiritual, if we will only avail ourselves of them.

When we do so, it is helpful to reflect on the fact that our bodies are what connect us to creation and to others as well as to God. Therefore, it is right that we should treasure our bodies and the bodies of others as well as creation and all God's creatures. The greater our sense of connection, the greater will be our love and appreciation for bodies of all kinds: big and little, abled and disabled, black and brown and yellow and white, human and animal, plant and mineral — even heavenly bodies!

This reverent love and appreciation for the physical as a means of communing with and offering service to God is at the heart of "sacramental" spirituality. The Orthodox, Catholic, and

Episcopal churches have retained some of this kind of spirituality, especially in worship. Today there is a widespread renewal of it in many parts of the worldwide church, due in part to the influence of ecumenical efforts that have allowed previously separated and even antagonistic Christians to lay aside their shameful divisions and learn to appreciate the riches in each other's traditions. Gradually, the spiritual arrogance of spiritual leaders on both sides of the Reformation divide is being overcome by a spirit of goodwill and a refreshing humility that sees the "log" in one's own eye (one's own tradition) instead of trying to pick out the speck in the others' eyes (other traditions)! Recent "spiritual" literature from many different parts of the Christian tradition reflects the growing common understanding of the urgent need for and advantages of "sacramental" spirituality.

In the current liturgical renewal movement, many churches are teaching sacramental spirituality as part of worship. As their members learn to reverence a certain place as holy or to embrace a range of things — water, candles, oil, bread, wine, incense, icons, sacred art, sacred music — as means of communion with God, the attitude of reverence taught toward these things spills over into reverence for the water they drink at home or swim in at the lake, the food they eat during ordinary meals, the candles they light for dinner, the art they create or buy to beautify their homes and churches, and the music they listen to every day.

As we learn to "tune in" to God with our bodies, we can sense God's presence in the glory of a sunflower, a sunset, or a symphony, or in the smell of fresh-baked bread, budding roses, and fragrant pines. With practice, we can, if we are mindful and reverent, commune with God in such a way that every meal is holy communion, every shower or bath a kind of baptism, every interaction with creation a high-priestly offering of thanks and praise to the Creator. Even a nap can become falling asleep in the arms of God. Our daily tasks can become an "offering of our bodies as a living sacrifice, holy and acceptable to God — our reasonable service" (Rom. 12:1).

We can also listen to God speaking to us through our bodies. Our senses are conduits of messages from God, letting us know when we are overloaded, when we need to stop and rest, when we need to enter into joy, when we need to attend to something causing pain or dis-ease. In the same way, God speaks to us through the bodies of others — through their beauty, their vulnerability, their need. If we really see them, as well as our own bodies, as the sanctuaries of the Holy Spirit, we will show appreciation, even reverence, for them. We will stop abusing any body, realizing that to do so is far worse than vandalizing a church building. And we will courageously confront and resist those who do act like vandals!

Moreover, when we really see the environment around us for what it is — the holy sanctuary of God's presence — we will be able to worship God in and through it and resist all those who would exploit it as if they were its owners. We will smell, taste, touch, see, and hear our way into God's presence far more often every day, and we will find that the milk and honey we take in through these experiences is rich and tasty indeed!

❊   ❊   ❊

Here are some specific "spiritual exercises" to help you further explore the material in this chapter and integrate it into your life:

1. In as beautiful a place as you can find, take a slow, "sensing" walk alone or with a friend who will walk in silence with you. During the walk, consciously commune with God, enjoying what you experience by focusing on each of your five senses one at a time. Write down what you experienced in your journal.

2. Eat at least one meal as if it were "holy communion." Using all of your senses, be as aware as possible of the food and the act of eating. Eat slowly and prayerfully, with a thankful spirit. Reflect on your experience in your journal.

3. During a shower or bath, meditate on its meaning as a reminder of your baptism, and of water as a means of communion with God's cleansing, refreshing love. Allow your body to enter as fully as possible into your experience with the water. Reflect on your experience in your journal.

4. Set aside a special "prayer time" to "tune in" to your body. Start by doing *lectio* with Romans 12:1-2; during the silence at the end (step 4), have a dialogue with your body and ask it to speak to you and tell you what you need to hear. Be open and playful about this (yes, you'll be using your imagination, and that's good!), and write down the dialogue in your journal — you can use art too, if you like.
5. For one day, try consciously relating to other people you meet as sacred sanctuaries of the Holy Spirit; try to show a special reverence for them, as you would for a beautiful cathedral.
6. On another day, try relating to animals, trees, flowers, and/or other creations of God as if each were an incredible masterpiece of the Greatest Artist of all. What does each one communicate about its Creator? Again, relate your experience in your journal.

Books for Further Reference

1. *Prayer and Our Bodies* by Flora S. Wuellner
   This wise contemporary author offers good guidance and practical exercises for exploring how to pray with our senses and our bodies. In this little gem of a book she gives many personal examples to illustrate her ideas and to inspire the reader.

2. *Pray All Ways* and *Secular Sanctity* by Edward Hays
   These two charming and practical books show how many overlooked ways there are for us to pray with our senses and in our surroundings "all ways." They open the door wide for many people who simply haven't realized how many ways there are to pray.

3. *On Becoming a Musical, Mystical Bear: Spirituality American Style* by Matthew Fox
   This is one of Fox's earliest books, in which he explores what a sensual American spirituality might look like, and why we need it. His writing is thought-provoking, untraditional, and lots of fun to read.

4. *Sadhana: A Way to God: Christian Exercises in Eastern Form*
   by Anthony de Mello
   This Catholic retreat master and spiritual director from India
   devotes this entire little book to exercises for prayer. He places
   great emphasis on praying with our bodies and on relishing the
   sacredness of the physical as a way to commune with God. This
   is a book I would want with me if I were alone for a long time
   on a remote desert island!

CHAPTER 5

The Wine of the Spirit: Dreams and Visions

When the Holy Spirit was poured out at Pentecost, the women and men who had gathered to wait for the fulfillment of Jesus' promise to send the Spirit were so inspired with dreams and visions, so full of prophecy and praises, that many of the people who came to hear them thought they were filled with new wine! (Acts 2).

Wine is a prominent feature of the Feast of God as it is described in Scripture. Wisdom offers wine at her table. Wisdom has sent out her servants; "she calls from the highest places in the town": "Come, eat of my bread and drink of the wine I have mixed. Lay aside immaturity, and live, and walk in the way of insight" (Prov. 9:3, 5-6). Isaiah the prophet speaks of a feast of wine offered by God on the "mountain of the Lord" (25:6).

During the wedding feast at Cana, Jesus turns large jars of water into gallons and gallons of the best wine (John 2). He offers wine to his disciples at the Last Supper and tells them he will not drink it again with his followers until the day when he drinks it "new" with them in his Abba's kingdom (Matt. 26:29).

At Pentecost, Peter assures the crowd that what they mistakenly think is the result of too much wine is, in fact, the fulfillment of Joel's prophecy that the gift of the Holy Spirit would be accompanied by dreams, visions, and prophecy by men and women, old and young, even slaves (Acts 2). It seems that wine is a fitting symbol for dreams and visions. Both access the unconscious and can therefore cause a change in consciousness, a lessening of inhibitions, and a change in behavior. No wonder many of the onlookers at Pentecost were confused!

While too much wine is damaging to human beings, the dreams and visions given by the Holy Spirit heal, help, and guide us. That is why Scripture says, "Do not be foolish, but understand what the will of the Lord is. Do not get drunk with wine, for that is debauchery; but be filled with the Spirit" (Eph. 5:17-18).

Scripture is filled with stories of how God's Spirit has spoken to people through the ages through dreams and visions, culminating with the outpouring of the Holy Spirit upon all flesh at Pentecost. God spoke to Abraham in visions both during the night and during the day, promising the birth of a son through whom all the nations of the earth would be blessed (Gen. 15, 18). God spoke to Hagar in the desert through a vision of an angel, guiding her to life-saving water for Ishmael and promising her a multitude of descendants as well (Gen. 16, 21). As Jacob fled from his brother's wrath, God came to him in a dream of angels climbing up and down a staircase that connected earth to heaven (Gen. 28). Joseph was given dreams that were a guide to his future, and later he was granted the gift of interpreting the dreams of others with great wisdom.

The prophetic books are filled with accounts of dreams and visions, and Daniel, like Joseph, was given the gift of interpreting the dreams of others as well. The dreams and visions continue into the New Testament. Angels visited both Mary and Joseph in dreams and visions; the wise men were warned in a dream not to return to Herod; Peter saw a vision on a rooftop in Joppa that changed his attitude about Gentiles; Paul saw a vision of Jesus on the road to Damascus that changed his life forever; and John saw visions on the island of Patmos that are described in the book of Revelation.

"Revelation" is an apt title for a book about dreams and visions, for that is just what many of them are: revelations from God for the benefit of those who received them. This is clearly the view of Scripture, and we need to take it seriously.

58

Of course, there are many different kinds of dreams, and not all of them are equally important or contain messages from God that are crucial for us. Some of our dreams are simply a processing of "stuff" that we've experienced that day or recently. Often these dreams aren't particularly memorable, and if we recall them at all in the morning, we remember only fragments of them. Such dreams often contain, for example, little snippets from something we saw on television or in a movie, a conversation we had, or something we heard in passing.

A second type of dream is more significant — the kind that reveals an ongoing issue in our lives that we need to deal with. Often this dream will reveal a perspective or an aspect of our lives that we haven't been sufficiently aware of. Sometimes the same dream, or a similar version of it, will come to us again and again, like a persistent knock on the door of our consciousness.

For example, several years ago when I was a more-than-full-time senior pastor, I began to have dreams about neglected children in my basement. My own children were grown by this time, so I came to realize that these neglected children represented parts of myself that I was ignoring and that needed attention: my body's need for more rest, my desire to write and paint, and my longing to spend more time in prayerful silence and solitude. It is an awful thing to neglect children, and these dreams let me know in no uncertain terms what I was doing to these God-given aspects of myself.

King Nebuchadnezzar's dream about the tree in Daniel 4 is a biblical example of this kind of dream. The king was becoming inflated with pride, but was not conscious of it or of its danger. The dream warned him about this issue in his life — an issue that everyone with great power must deal with head-on because of power's ability to corrupt.

A third type of dream is the kind that is incredibly vivid and leaves one with a feeling of awe. It is a numinous dream, mysterious and powerful and profoundly spiritual. Such a dream is unforgettable and often seems more real than one's waking experiences. In fact, such a dream can change one's life as much as or more than a significant waking experience. Sometimes such dreams spark an invention or a creation that has great significance. It is

COME TO THE FEAST

said, for instance, that many of Marc Chagall's paintings were inspired by dreams. Scripture is full of such dreams, for they are usually the kind in which God most clearly speaks. Angels often appear in them, as in the dream Jacob had at Bethel, and the dream Joseph had when he was pondering whether or not to marry Mary because she was pregnant before they had relations.

Dreams, of course, are what we experience while we are sleeping. Visions, on the other hand, whether sought or unsought, usually come while we are awake. They are vivid mind-pictures that we see with the "inner eye." Like dreams, they reveal something about the past or present or future, and often what is going on under the surface or behind the scenes. The visions of the prophets and John the apostle were of this kind: they revealed through symbolic language the spiritual meaning of historical events, and they revealed messages from God clothed in symbolic form — like the beasts in Daniel's visions (Dan. 7); the wheels in the air that Ezekiel saw (Ezek. 1); and the woman, the child, and the dragon of John's vision (Rev. 12).

Sometimes visions are a clear form of call and guidance, like the visions Paul had when he was on the road to Damascus and when he was on one of his missionary journeys (Acts 9, 16). Like dreams, visions are not rare, nor are they limited to biblical times or cultures. The annals of history and literature and the accounts of anthropologists contain many descriptions of the visions and dreams that people have had.

For example, Thomas Aquinas, the famous Catholic saint and philosopher, had a divine vision near the end of his life which, he said, led him to stop writing, because the vision made all his writing seem like so much straw. Hildegard of Bingen, another famous Christian leader and teacher, had an entire series of visions that she called illuminations. She described them to an artist-scribe, who recorded them, and she wrote meditations based on them as well.

Visions and dreams are quite different from rational, discursive thought. They speak in a language all their own — the symbolic language of poetry and art. They are made up of images that act as symbols. A symbol expresses an invisible and formless spiritual reality in a concrete physical image that fits it.

The elements of the Eucharist, for example, bring together the invisible, spiritual reality of Christ's presence and its outward expression in the bread and wine. Similarly, the water of baptism is a symbol that brings water together with its inner spiritual meaning — that of cleansing and refreshing, the quenching of thirst, and the giving of life. This understanding of the wedding of inner and outer reality through the use of symbols is profoundly explored in the Gospel of John — for example, in Jesus' conversation with the Samaritan woman about the Water of Life, and in Jesus' discourses on the Bread of Life and Living Water (John 4, 6, and 7). The parables of Jesus are further evidence of the power of concrete stories and images to convey spiritual meanings.

The crucial thing about interpreting symbols, especially those in dreams and visions, is not to take them literally, as we have seen in the examples described so far in this chapter. They are to be explored for what meanings and associations they have for the dreamer and the dreamer's culture. (I'll say more about this later.) This approach assumes that dreams have meaning — and, in fact, spiritual and psychological meaning.

This is precisely what the early church fathers believed about dreams and visions. During the first four to five centuries of Christianity, dreams and visions were regarded as a means through which God and the angels communicated with people, and therefore as a part of God's providence. For example, Cyprian, the bishop of Carthage in 250 A.D., claimed that the councils of the church were guided by God through dreams and visions. He also wrote a great deal about his own direct encounters with God in dreams and visions.

Other Christian writers and teachers also recognized dreams and visions as containing symbols that revealed the nature of the spiritual world. Tertullian, conservative though he was, said that the great majority of human beings get their knowledge of God from dreams. The prevailing opinion in those early centuries was that dreams presented people with what they needed to know to fulfill God's plan for their lives. They helped people communicate with the inner, invisible spiritual world, which was considered fully as real as the outer world known by the senses and the truths known by reason.

Unfortunately, when Christianity became the official religion, and when people became Christians without real commitment or solid grounding in Christian teaching, dreams and visions became suspect. Popular and pagan superstitions and practices linked dreams and visions to fortune-telling and divination. Among many Christians, dream work degenerated into a self-centered way of predicting the future and trying to increase power, pleasure, wealth, and/or health. Dream work as a discipline of spiritual growth into holiness and wholeness was forgotten except among a few holy men and women in the church.

Because dreams and visions had become popular tools of magic and superstition, at least in the West, the Latin church leaders cautioned strongly against paying attention to dreams and visions, urging instead a faith in the doctrines of the church. However, the original tradition favoring dreams and visions as revelations from God continued through Basil the Great, Saint Gregory, and John Chrysostom in the Eastern Orthodox Church, which historically has placed more spiritual value on dreams and visions.

Although he himself had a couple of remarkable and life-changing dreams and visions, Saint Thomas Aquinas, in trying to integrate the thought of Aristotle with the teachings of Christianity, took Aristotle's position that dreams had merely natural causes and were of little value. This view prevailed in Western Christianity, aided centuries later by the scientific mind-set which denied that anything true and real could be known except through the physical senses, through reason, and through scientific experiment.

It wasn't until the twentieth century, especially the latter half of it, that the early church's tradition and the biblical point of view about dreams and visions began to be recovered. A whole array of Christian thinkers from various parts of the Christian tradition have been rediscovering and exploring the value of visions and dreams for spiritual growth. Two of the most influential pioneers in this movement have been Morton Kelsey and John Sanford. Both of them are pastors and psychologists, and both have a keen interest in the close relationship between spirituality and psychology. Morton Kelsey's book entitled *The Other Side of Silence,* which has become a classic in the field, lays a philosophical and theological foundation for the use of dreams and visions in prayer and meditation for spiritual growth. John Sanford's book entitled *Dreams: God's Forgotten Language* is a convincing study of the biblical material on dreams and visions; Sanford has also included many contemporary illustrations from his counseling experience which indicate that dreams and visions have functioned in modern people's lives in the same way they did in the lives of biblical figures.

These and other works would seem to indicate that the dreams and visions that are the wine of the Holy Spirit are still being poured out for us at the Banqueting Table to which God invites us. Because of the negative attitudes toward dreams and visions that have prevailed for centuries in church and society, it is a helpful "balancing act" for us to consider the advantages of drinking this wine of the Spirit at the Feast.

The first advantage of dreams and visions is that they are a great help in discerning our hidden faults, our secret sins, and the aspects of ourselves we would rather not see. All of us have only a partial view of ourselves. This view is based on personal experience, what others have told us we are like, how they have treated us, and the conclusions we have drawn. "Confession is good for the soul," says the ancient proverb. Our dreams and visions can be a great help in providing us with material for more complete confession. Of course, God doesn't need the information! But we do. Because our dreams and visions provide us with material from the unconscious, they inform us of things we need to know about ourselves, some of which are dark and destructive. Anger, hatred, fear, despair, pride, and more are buried in the depths of our beings.

Someone I know, for instance, had a dream about throwing the head of a leader down from a castle tower onto the ground below. When she pondered the dream and what was going on in her life, she realized how angry she was with someone in her church who had been sabotaging her in various ways. She had been trying to be "nice" to him anyway, and had buried her true feelings deep inside. When she realized how angry she really was with him, she spent time processing that in prayer, offering her anger to God and asking for guidance so that she could handle her relationship with this man more honestly. After doing this, she felt a great sense

63

of relief. She also found an opportunity to let the man know how she really felt and to ask him to be more supportive of her.

Sometimes dreams and visions will also reveal the presence of an inner enemy, a critical, negative person who appears in dreams in various guises. The presence of this figure reveals clearly that there is a self-sabotaging dynamic within us that needs to be confronted and healed. As long as it remains in our unconscious, it will do us in one way or another, and we won't even realize what's happening. This negative figure in dreams and visions can represent both an internal criticism and a kind of societal criticism. For example, many women have dreams that involve negative male figures. When a woman has this kind of dream, the male may be a kind of tyrant who is constantly finding fault with her and often attacks her in some way. This figure represents a critical aspect of herself. He is often very much like a father or another male in her life whom the woman has perceived as critical and domineering. This figure may also represent the negative attitudes toward women that are common in society, attitudes that many women have internalized.

Once we become conscious of such an inner enemy, we can bring it in prayer to God; and we can dialogue with it, just as Jesus did with the Tempter in the wilderness, and let it know that we will not heed its critical voice anymore. (John Sanford has a great deal more to say about this confessional advantage of dreams in many of his books, two of which are listed in the bibliography.)

A second advantage of listening to our dreams and visions is that they are frequently a way in which we receive divine guidance and warning. Biblical examples of these kinds of dreams include the dream that the Magi had after Jesus was born, warning them to return home a different way, and the dream Joseph had warning him to flee to Egypt with Mary and Jesus.

A common dream that people in our society have is "the car dream": they are going somewhere in their car, and it runs out of gas, or gets stuck, or breaks down in a dangerous place. In this dream, the car often symbolizes the psychic space or situation of the dreamer, and the car problems are warnings that the dreamer is taking a course that will end in trouble. I had a series of dreams like this several years ago, when I was overloading and overworking myself. But I didn't heed the message of those dreams, and a short time later, I became ill. If I had believed then, as I do now, that dreams do contain divine guidance, I would have taken their message more seriously, even if it had involved making some difficult choices and changes.

Sometimes dreams will affirm rather than warn a person about a choice they have made, especially if they are still having some inner doubts about it. A friend of mine decided after considerable struggle to take the risk of giving up a job that no longer fulfilled her in favor of a career in art. Even though she was happy about her decision, she kept wondering if she had made the right choice. Then she dreamt that she was a woman about to give birth. In the dream, she felt full of joy at the prospect, although, like most women, a bit apprehensive about the hard labor involved. This dream confirmed her direction so clearly that her doubts dissipated, and she pursued her new direction with much greater confidence.

The dream that Jacob had when he was fleeing from Esau was also an affirming dream. It revealed a gracious God who was with him in spite of his deception and fear. It gave him the confidence to go on to a strange new land and try to make a life for himself there. Indeed, the dream was so vivid and wonderful that Jacob never forgot it, and he passed the story of his dream on to his children.

A third advantage of dreams and visions is that they contribute significantly to our wholeness and the integration of our personalities. They speak with the voice of a Wisdom far greater than our own. Sometimes they will reveal gifts we have but are unaware of, or present challenges to do something we would never have consciously chosen to do. This is certainly what happened to Paul, who would never have chosen to serve Jesus as an apostle to the Gentiles if it had not been for his vision on the road to Damascus. Because Paul was faithful and obedient to that vision, the whole course of salvation history was changed.

Most of us won't have such an obvious or profound effect on history. But to the extent that we hear and follow the Wisdom that the Holy Spirit provides through dreams and visions, we will blossom in ways we never would or could otherwise. Inventors, poets, artists, and musicians know, as do many saints, that their greatest accomplishments are inspired from depths beyond their "normal" consciousness. In fact, each of us has a great deal of untapped talent, potential, and wisdom that lies beyond our current level of awareness.

If we desire the wisdom to become all that God means us to be, we will often find it in the dreams and visions that come to us: they will help us discern new gifts and directions, and offer new insights to help us become more whole and grow in integrity. Sometimes this wisdom also speaks to us about our relationships and ways we can be more honest, loving, and helpful in them. There are other times when the wisdom that comes to us indicates that we need to remove ourselves from a relationship that is destructive and oppressive so that we can be healed and flourish.

One of my daughters had just such a dream while she was in a relationship with a young man with whom she was very much in love. During a vacation when they were spending a great deal of time together, she began to have an intuition that something wasn't right, but she didn't want to admit her feelings. Then one night she dreamt that he was trying to strangle her! When she awoke and meditated on the dream, she realized that it was telling her in urgent terms what he was doing to her in a subtle way by treating her in a patronizing and demeaning manner. Shortly after she had this dream she had the good sense to end the relationship.

Healing is a fourth important advantage of heeding our dreams and visions. When we do, they help us develop the wholeness that is God's will for us. One tried-and-true way to tap into this healing power is by using our imaginations to envision Jesus or the Holy Spirit's Light in a painful past memory, and letting the Divine Presence change it into a good one. Or we can imagine someone we love and trust deeply acting as an instrument of God's love in the memory. In many Christian circles this is called "healing of the memories," and it is a powerful way to resolve old hurts and griefs.

Another especially effective approach is to enter imaginatively into Bible stories, especially those in the Gospels. By identifying with someone who is healed by Jesus, and reliving that healing imaginatively in vivid detail as if it were our own, we can experience a profound healing of both body and soul.

There are many other ways in which dreams and visions contribute to our healing and wholeness as well. Sometimes they will warn us in a symbolic way of the presence of a disease developing within us of which we are unaware. Sometimes they will give us clues about the kind of healing process that would be best for us.

Even when we don't remember our dreams, God restores both body and soul during sleep, refreshing our physical selves with rest, and helping us through dreams to "work through" and process what is going on in our lives. Dream researchers tell us that when people are consistently wakened as they enter the dream phase of sleep, which is signaled by REM (rapid eye movement), they begin after a number of dreamless nights to exhibit all the symptoms of serious mental breakdown. It is now well established that dreaming is essential to sanity and well-being.

It is fortunate for us that Christian leaders such as Agnes Sanford, Matthew and Dennis Linn, Flora Wuellner, and Morton Kelsey have all pioneered ways of experiencing healing through meditating on dreams (which they teach us how to remember) and actively using our imaginations. These methods offer us a way to redeem the evil and heal the wounds in our past that still fester deep inside us, and profoundly affect our emotions, attitudes, and behavior in the present.

A fifth advantage of dreams and visions is their ability to energize us and help us become more creative. Imaging is an important part of the creative process. The spiritual depths sounded by dreams and visions are the same depths that give birth to great creations in music and art and great ideas in science and philosophy. Because spirituality and creativity are closely intertwined, dreams and visions can be important resources for creativity in our lives.

Handel is said to have experienced a visionary state as he composed *The Messiah* in a rush of creative inspiration. Lewis Carroll admitted that his inspiration for *Alice in Wonderland* came from a dream. Many famous painters, like Marc Chagall, have drawn upon dream images and visionary experiences in their

67

greatest art. The examples could be multiplied, but personal experience is what will truly convince us of the marvelous well of energy and creativity from which we can draw by listening to our dreams and using our imaginations.

The sixth and final advantage of dreams and visions is that they provide us with a wonderful way to pray, to meditate, and to be profoundly connected with the life and wisdom of the Holy Spirit, who, according to the Bible, has been poured out into our hearts and dwells in our beings. Through our imaginations, active in dreams when we are asleep and in visions when we are awake, we exercise one of our unique capacities as image-bearers of God — that is, the capacity to develop mental images and create all kinds of things.

While it is true that our imaginations, like the rest of our beings, are fallen, and can be occasions for stumbling into fear or despair or foolish and destructive behavior, it is also true that our imaginations, along with every other part of us, have been redeemed and set free from the power of sin by the saving acts of God in and through Jesus Christ. When we open ourselves wholeheartedly to the sanctifying presence of the Holy Spirit, we can trust that her voice will speak to us from within dreams and visions as well as through Scripture and outer experiences. The whole New Testament bears witness to this wonderful truth, which we in our generation are just beginning to appreciate anew.

Moreover, these days we have the benefit of much pioneering work done by pastors, counselors, and theologians to help us not only realize the advantages of dreams and visions but also learn how to enter into them, and in a prayerful way to discover the messages in them for us. The following brief descriptions of some of these methods are not intended to give you all you need to know before you drink in the dreams and visions that are the Wine of the Spirit at the great Banqueting Table. Rather, they are intended to whet your appetite for these sources and others, so that you will learn enough about the Wine to truly appreciate it and drink it wisely and well.

In order to work with your dreams, it is vitally important to get a notebook to use as your dream journal. The best kind has unlined pages, so you can draw the images you remember, if you like, as well as write them down. Keep your journal near your bed, along with a pencil and a pen. Just doing this, with the desire and intention to remember your dreams, will aid in your dream recall.

When you are ready to sleep, prayerfully ask the Holy Spirit to help you remember what you need to from your dreams. When you awake in the morning (or if you can't get back to sleep during the night), write down anything you remember from your dreams right away — even if it's only a fragment or a mood or a question. Recording whatever you can remember is your way of taking a step of faith.

In *Dreams and Spiritual Growth*, the authors offer a helpful way to "mine" a dream: it's called the TTAQ (Title–Theme–Affect–Question) method. Once you've written down what you can remember of a dream, give it a title. Let it come to you spontaneously or ask yourself, "What title does this dream want to have?" Next, state the major theme or issue that surfaced in the dream. If there is more than one, note them in sequence. Then note the dominant feeling or emotional energy you experienced during the dream. If you experienced a sequence of feelings, state them in sequence. Finally, write down what question(s) the dream may be asking of you. What is the dream trying to help you become conscious of?[1]

A second fruitful dream-work technique is to dialogue with a dream figure. *Dreams and Spiritual Growth* gives these directions for this technique:

1. Choose some character, figure or image from your dream for dialogue. Select one that seems prominent or important to you, either one you want to approach, or one you would rather avoid.

2. Make sure it is a time and a place where you will not be interrupted. Let yourself relax, place yourself in a meditative attitude, and in your own way welcome God's presence and guidance as you begin your dream work dialogue.

1. Louis M. Savary et al., *Dreams and Spiritual Growth: A Christian Approach to Dreamwork* (Mahwah, N.J.: Paulist Press, 1984), p. 24.

3. Using your imagination, recreate the dream scene where your chosen figure appeared. Let the dream figure come alive again for you. If the figure is a symbol such as a torch, key, house, cloud, car, painting, mountain, or breeze, personify or name the figure in such a way that you can enter into dialogue with it.

4. Begin with a few opening questions to get the relationship started. Write down your first question, and in your imagination picture yourself asking it to your dream figure.

5. Then write whatever response seems to come to you as the dream figure's reply. Let your pen move spontaneously as you write, not caring about grammar, spelling, or punctuation.

6. Continue the dialogue until you feel something has been changed or resolved, an insight has been gained, or until you want or need to stop. The dialogue itself is a gift.

7. When the dialogue seems to be coming to a natural closing, we recommend you ask one last question — "Do you have anything else to tell me or give me?" — just in case something important has been forgotten.

8. After the dialogue, reflect on what happened, perhaps taking a few minutes to reread and dialogue and find a Title, Theme, Affect and Question for it. Find some way to clarify the energy and insight that may have been communicated to you, and propose ways you might use this gift in your daily life.[2]

In her book *Awakening,* Dr. Ellen Foreman offers the following additional helpful observations about dreams:

> The idea is to allow dreams to speak in their own language — through their own images, structure, and logic — and to treat them like other products of imagination — like works of art, poems, and plays. Dreams are intricate works of beauty, elegance, and complexity, not codes to be reduced to a simplistic message. Dreams have meaning on many levels simultaneously, and the longer you work on a dream, the more it has to offer you. . . .

2. Savary et al., *Dreams and Spiritual Growth,* pp. 62-63.

The dream you are most likely to remember will be the last dream of the night, which usually occurs just before you normally wake up. When you awaken from a dream, lie still and play it back, letting its images make their impression on your mind. . . . If you have a "feeling" of a dream without its images or story, try shifting your body, simulating various sleep positions. Dreams seem to surface in the position in which they were dreamed, as if the body contained the memory. To trigger the memories, try thinking about significant people in your life, or of yesterday's events, or of current problems you are facing.

Write your dreams down as soon as you have replayed them. . . . To preserve their immediacy, record your dreams in the present tense with as much detail as you can recall. . . . Try to record the events in chronological order, to preserve the structure of the dream. Sometimes a color in the dream, or whether the dream is in color, is important and should be noted. If there are powerful images that are hard to describe, use the margins of your journal to draw them. . . .

In writing the dream, let the words spill out spontaneously. Let the flow of the dream carry you on. Sometimes you will find yourself having difficulty finding the right word. This is important. Give yourself time to find the word that fits most precisely. One dreamer recorded, "I found myself lost on city blocks." She used "blocks," instead of "streets," and that choice felt very important to her. In interpreting her dream, she realized it was the key: the dream was about feeling blocked. Use a word even if it feels strange to you. Don't correct it. It may be very significant. Where one dreamer might ordinarily have described his situation as "living on a hill," he found himself writing, "living on a bluff." Indeed, he discovered that he felt he was being fraudulent in his professional life. Our dreams often use puns that can provide us with the key to their meaning. . . .

At the center of every dream lies a conflict hidden from waking life, an unresolved problem. Most of the dreams that we remember spontaneously are highly charged emotionally and occur at times that are most stressful. Dream research shows that the more conflicts we are experiencing in our daytime life, the more dream sleep we need. The dreams are attempts to resolve the conflicts. They offer new perspectives, which we may not be aware of in waking life. The conflict expresses itself as a theme in the dream. . . . If you can connect the conflict in a dream's theme with a real-life conflict, you have a key to the dream's meaning and, more important, keys to understanding and resolving a major issue in your life.[3]

Finally, I recommend the following three-step way to work with dreams that is suggested by Robert Johnson in *Inner Work*; this is the method that I have personally found most helpful.

A. Log your dream

1. Center yourself in God and ask the Holy Spirit's wisdom in remembering and discerning whatever wisdom may be meant for you in the dream.

2. Everything in a dream is symbolic, not logical. Each person or thing or action is a metaphor with its own special meaning. Write down as many of the important or vivid things, persons, and actions in the dream as you can remember.

B. Interpret elements of the dream

1. Now think about each element of the dream individually and write down whatever comes to mind in "free association" style.

2. Consider the dynamics of the dream — the action pattern — and see if it connects with any dynamics going on in your life right now.

3. Write down any insights you now have into the dream's meaning for your life.

4. Act on them: do something concrete, even physical, to integrate the insights into your life.

3. Foreman, *Awakening: A Dream Journal,* 2 vols. (New York: Stewart, Tabori & Chang, 1988), pp. 16, 22, 24, 35, 38.

C. *Test your interpretation*

1. Does your interpretation show you something you didn't already know or knew only faintly? Does it challenge your existing ideas? If so, it's probably right. Usually dreams don't tell us what's obvious; they tell us what we need to know and aren't "getting." Sometimes dreams will repeat themselves in various ways to get our attention if there is something important we need to realize. When dreams repeat themselves, they merit special attention!

2. Is your interpretation egotistical or self-serving? Does it condone actions or attitudes toward others or yourself that might be damaging or disrespectful? In that case, it's probably a misinterpretation. On the other hand, if your interpretation is consistent with the fruits of the Holy Spirit, you can accept its wisdom with confidence. (See Galatians 5:16-25.)

3. Does your interpretation shift responsibility away from you? That's probably another sign of a misinterpretation. Usually your dreams aren't concerned with the faults of other people or their need to change. That's between them and God. Your dreams are usually concerned with you and *your* need to live a fully aware and responsible life.

4. How does your interpretation fit with your interpretations of other dreams? Live with your dream over a period of time and look for similar patterns in other dreams. Most of your dreams have to do with what's currently going on in your life. But there are "big dreams" too — especially vivid ones that reveal the "big picture" in your life and carry an especially important message. These are more rare, the kind of dreams we find recorded in Scripture. Sometimes they have as much to do with the deeper spiritual issues of society as they do with your personal life. Of course, the two are connected, so you can expect the connection to show in your dreams.

It's important to remember that you are the best interpreter of your own dreams, and that no one should impose an interpretation on anyone else's dreams. Sometimes, however, other wise individuals who have done a great deal of their own dream work can offer a perspective that will help you see the blind spot in your own approach to a dream. Such persons are invaluable.[4]

✵   ✵   ✵

Visions, in contrast to dreams, are usually what you experience "with your eyes wide open." You are awake and aware, although experiencing an altered state of consciousness. You ask for the Holy Spirit's protection and guidance, and then you wait for whatever visual images may arise in your mind. You can fully participate as yourself in the imaginary experience, noting your thoughts and feelings, asking questions, and, most of all, listening to the message in the vision for you. It is important that you stay focused during this process by writing down what is happening. (Drawing can also be valuable as a response to and a record of your vision.)

The images that will be given to you will be unique to your personality, experience, and imagination. They will reveal a great deal to you if you let them. Sometimes a story unfolds in a vision, with a plot as well as characters. At other times a vision is simply a scene and a dialogue. (The biblical stories of the visions of the prophets are examples of this.) As I noted earlier, this kind of visionary experience abounds with symbolic figures, not with people from your everyday life.

Sometimes it is helpful to enter into an imaginary experience with someone else as your assistant. You tell him or her what you are experiencing; then she or he helps you by asking questions about what you see, hear, feel, sense, smell, and so on. This is another technique that can help you stay focused on the experience, so long as the other person doesn't intrude with his or her own interpretations or ideas. This technique also functions as a safeguard against becoming overwhelmed by a powerful imaginary experience. This isn't common, but if it does happen, it's good to have someone to turn to who can help you "come to your senses" and get grounded again.

4. Johnson, *Inner Work: Using Dreams and Active Imagination for Personal Growth* (New York: Harper & Row, 1986), pp. 51-134.

Getting grounded also involves actually *doing* something to honor the message of the dream or vision. Sometimes it means making a concrete change in your behavior, attitudes, or plans. At other times, it means creating a ritual that will honor the message. Isaiah's vision in the temple, for example (Isaiah 6), called for concrete action: Isaiah's going to God's people with God's message. Mary went to her cousin Elizabeth to process her vision and its meaning for her life. Jacob built an altar of stones to honor his vision of angels. As these biblical examples show, it is vitally important to always integrate the meaning and message in dreams and visions into your life as concretely as possible. Otherwise you are playing games, and that is a dangerous thing to do in the spiritual realm.

Still another way of using your imagination for spiritual growth and healing is the time-honored way offered by the spiritual exercises of St. Ignatius, and methods adapted from these exercises, such as those found in *Healing Life's Hurts* (listed in the "Books for Further Reference" section at the end of this chapter). These exercises can guide you into imagining yourself as a participant in stories in the Gospels or other parts of Scripture. It helps to do this kind of imagining by enlisting the help of another person who can listen and ask questions, as described above, or by writing down in a journal what you're experiencing as you experience it. There is great power in biblical stories, especially those in the Gospels, and if you will enter into them with faith and imagination, you can open yourself up to amazing grace indeed!

Finally, there is the way of the artist: You can create something visible with clay or wood, paint or pencil, movement or music — something that expresses your inner dreams and visions, your imagination's creative powers, and makes what you think, feel, sense, hear, and imagine visible or audible. This "objectifies" your inner experience and allows you to have further dialogue with it.

❀   ❀   ❀

All of these ways, and many more, provide us with the opportunity to drink in the "Wine" of visions and dreams for our spiritual nourishment and well-being. Like wine, they are powerful and consciousness-altering, and so they need to be treated with great respect and moderation. A little wine is good for the soul as well as the stomach; too much can be overwhelming. Each person who comes to the Table needs to discern how much of the Wine of dreams and visions is "enough" for him or her.

It is good, too, to drink in the company of others. "Drinking" within the context of the communion of the saints and soliciting the wise listening and support of one or more people who are experienced in working with dreams and visions are ways to guard against the kinds of excesses and mistakes that gave dreams and visions a bad name in the church after Christianity became the official state religion.

Finally, a certain amount of maturity and a rootedness in the wisdom of classic religious traditions, along with a robust trust in God, are important if we want to enjoy the Wine that God pours out for us through the Holy Spirit's presence deep within us.

✸ ✸ ✸

Here are some specific spiritual exercises to help you further explore the material in this chapter and integrate it into your life:

1. Select and reflect upon at least two biblical stories of dreams or visions. Then write down your reflections and what you learned from them in your journal.
2. Using some of the techniques described in this chapter, work with a past or recent dream that you remember well. Write down the dream's message to you and your response to it.
3. Try one of the ways of actively using your imagination in a "visionary" way: by reliving a memory so that it is transformed, by extending a dream imaginatively, by simply letting images come to mind, or by entering into a Bible story. Do this exercise with a partner if you can, especially if you have any anxiety about it. If you decide to do this exercise alone, be sure you write and/or draw as you go through the experience.

4. Express a dream or a visionary/imaginative experience in some visible or audible way (paint, draw, weave, carve, sing, dance, play) and see what further wisdom this process yields for you.

Books for Further Reference

1. *The Other Side of Silence: A Guide to Christian Meditation* by Morton T. Kelsey
   This groundbreaking classic builds a firm theological basis for heeding dreams and visions. The author gives personal examples of how he has worked with his own dreams and visions and benefited from them.

2. *Dreams: God's Forgotten Language* by John A. Sanford
   The author, a pastor and counselor, lays a thorough biblical foundation for heeding dreams and gives many examples of how they contain important messages for us from a wise and loving God.

3. *Inner Work: Using Dreams and Active Imagination for Personal Growth* by Robert A. Johnson
   This book by a well-known therapist and lecturer provides a psychological basis for using dreams and active imagination for personal development. Johnson offers specific practical steps for working wisely and well with dreams and imagination.

4. *Dreams and Spiritual Growth: A Christian Approach to Dreamwork* by Louis M. Savary, Stephen Kaplan Williams, and Patricia H. Berne
   In this book the authors offer a helpful historical survey, biblical material, and many specific and creative dream-work techniques based on the numerous workshops they have led in dreams and spiritual growth.

5. *Healing Life's Hurts: Healing Memories through the Five Stages of Forgiveness* by Dennis and Matthew Linn

COME TO THE FEAST

This book has a workbook format so that it can be used either by pairs or by groups. It offers a wonderful array of exercises that are inspired by the Ignatian model but are more flexible and gentle in approach and also better suited to contemporary sensibilities. It deals extensively with healing memories by using imaginative prayer.

PART TWO

I devoted the first half of this book to describing the marvelous feast of spiritual food that God has prepared for all who will come to the Banqueting Table. How we are able, at this time in our lives, to choose, enjoy, and be nourished by these spiritual foods depends to a great extent on who we are right now as unique individuals. What we are able to take in physically varies tremendously: some people can't tolerate lactose and so cannot stomach milk; others are allergic to certain fruits or grains; and still others, out of deep conviction, will not eat meat. Just so, what we feast on at the Banqueting Table is influenced by our deeply held convictions, our past experience, and our present ability to be nourished by the various kinds of spiritual food that I have described.

I believe it is crucial for us to know ourselves as well as possible when we come to the Table. Too often in the past, spiritual leaders and writers urged certain spiritual disciplines upon people because they themselves had found the disciplines helpful. But as often as not, their suggestions didn't work for their followers, who would then conclude that they just weren't "spiritual enough" and that something was wrong with them. Many would simply give up the whole effort, not realizing that the problem lay not with them but with the spiritual nourishment they were being offered, which was simply not suited to them at that particular time in their lives.

At one point in my life, for example, I decided to try a form of the Ignatian spiritual exercises. I tried as hard as I could to follow the instructions in the book I had been given on the subject. But it all felt so structured, so confining, so alien to me that I finally gave up. Fortunately, by this time I had realized that what works for some people wonderfully well is not at all helpful to others. So I didn't despair of my spiritual potential. I simply went on to try other kinds of spiritual nourishment. The lesson here is clear: When you first come to the Table in an intentional manner, you need to give yourself time to experiment with the various foods being offered so that you can discover through personal experience what is best for your own nourishment.

When you undertake the process of discerning what is best for you, you need to include reflection upon some of the factors that most influence your choice of the spiritual food available to you: the family, the religious tradition, and the culture in which you have grown up; your temperament and personality; your age and stage in life; and your gender. The chapters that follow will explore each of these in turn, as a way of helping you discern what kind of spiritual nourishment is best for you at this point in your life.

CHAPTER 6

Formed by Family, Conditioned by Culture

The most important of all the influences on our lives, and therefore on our choices at the Banqueting Table, is that of our family, both immediate and extended. We can include in the term "family" any others who have been very close and influential in our lives and whose actions and attitudes have deeply affected us. They have influenced us on both conscious and unconscious levels.

Your image of God, for example, is inevitably shaped by your experience of your parents, especially your father, since God is most often named this way in the Christian tradition. The image of God you have in your heart will affect everything else: how you pray, or do not pray; how you feel about yourself and others; how you conduct your life. If you were mistreated as a child and learned not to trust, it will be very hard for you to genuinely trust God or listen to the depths of your heart in the belief that God the Holy Spirit resides there. It will also be hard for you to trust yourself and others, for that matter.

Unfortunately, it is hard for anyone shadowed by fear and suspicion to accept the spiritual nourishment that God offers. Trust is a crucial spiritual issue. You can let go of your fear only when you come to realize what you are projecting onto God based on your childhood experience. When you can let go of that, you can receive love from the true, tender God revealed by Jesus Christ.

Your parents are also models of faith (or the lack of it), so it is important for you to examine how what they taught by word and example influences what you can and cannot eat at the Table. If, for instance, your parents never prayed out loud with you and for you and, as far as you could tell, probably didn't pray personally in the context of a living and loving relationship with God, you will feel very differently about prayer than if you had faithful, prayerful parents. On the other hand, if one or both of your parents were full of pious talk and active in church while they were manipulative and even abusive at home, you will have a revulsion for anything that seems to be like their piety.

A person I know, for instance, was raised in a minister's home. As an adult, he found that whenever he was in church, he experienced a closed-in, suffocating feeling that was terrible. One day he went back into his childhood memories of church in an intense and intentional way, and he discovered how stifled he had felt in church as a little boy. Apparently he had been a lively child, and he remembered being frequently silenced or spanked by his parents, and being stared at disapprovingly by those around him. Naturally, this affected how he could receive the nourishment of worship in his life. He needed to go back to those early negative experiences and allow God to heal and change the bad memories, so that he would be free to experience worship in a new way as an adult. (For more on how this can happen, see Agnes Sanford's *The Healing Gifts of the Spirit.)*

The Bread of divine reading, especially the reading of Scripture, might be most nourishing to you if you as a child experienced Bible reading as delightful, interesting, and inspiring. But if Bible verses were often used as a club to squelch your questions, or put you in your place, or correct you in a manipulative way by making you feel guilty, it is unlikely that you will feel drawn to reading the Bible for spiritual nourishment.

I remember a time when my husband and I and our four small children were visiting some old friends. The couple also had small children, and when we had finished supper, the father interrupted the children's laughter and talk by saying sternly, "Sit down and shut up now! We've got to read the Bible!" I doubt that his children grew up to see the Bible as a source of delightful nourishment, like fresh homemade bread, warm from the oven.

82

In all of these ways and many more, your childhood family experience affects what you are able and willing to eat at the Feast of spiritual nourishment provided by God. The little child you once were lives on and comes to the Table with you, whether or not you know it or like it. To the extent that you become conscious of how you are presently influenced by your early family experiences, you are free to choose whether or not to let them bind you or blind you to the possibilities for your spiritual nourishment at the Banqueting Table.

In addition, what appeals to you at the Feast and what you can stomach is very much influenced by the religious tradition that most formed you. If you were shaped by the Reformed tradition, for instance, with its strong emphasis on the Word of God and the use of the intellect as a means of spiritual growth, the bread of *lectio divina* may be a food you would choose. On the other hand, the tradition's strong iconoclastic streak and its suspicion of emotion and the senses could make it difficult for you to worship in ways that are emotional, free, and spontaneous. You might also find it hard to enjoy the sacramental approach of Orthodoxy or the silence in worship practiced by Quakers.

Each of the major Christian traditions shapes those brought up in it in ways that make some of the foods at the Feast easier for them to digest than others. I know a Quaker woman, for example, who relishes silence with all her heart and finds typical Reformed worship far too wordy and rationalistic. On the other hand, one of my brothers, who is Russian Orthodox, needs the profoundly sacramental, sensuous, dramatic, and beautiful worship of the Orthodox tradition in order to feed his soul. In his case, it was precisely the absence of this sort of worship in his Reformed upbringing that drove him to seek a more physical spirituality in worship and prayer. His example reminds us that sometimes it is the lack of something in our own religious tradition which makes us hunger for something else. Many people who find themselves in different denominations at different points in their lives are where they are precisely because they need something that was missing from their previous experience.

The charismatic movement, which has established a presence in most denominations by now, has drawn many such people because it offers worship, prayer, and small-group experiences that honor the life of the Holy Spirit within, and the dreams and visions that are her gifts. Those who hunger for the direct, inner experience of God, and whose background has fed their minds more than their hearts, often find that the Wine of the Spirit is just what they need.

On the other hand, there are plenty of people who have been so ingrained by their upbringing to be skeptical of and even opposed to the charismatic approach that they find it very difficult to enjoy the Wine of the Spirit. The Bread of *lectio* suits them much better, along with the predictable and set forms of worship with which they are familiar.

Obviously, it is important for each of us to examine how our religious tradition has influenced our assumptions and to realize just why we may shy away from certain spiritual foods and be attracted to others. Such awareness can help to free us of unconscious limits and liberate us to decide whether or not we will allow our religious background to limit what food we eat at the Feast.

Last but not least, there is the influence of the society and culture in which we were raised. In a way, society and culture can be likened to what the ocean is for the fish who live in it. An old "fish story" tells of a young fish who swims up to a wise older fish and asks, "Where is this ocean I keep hearing about all the time?" The old fish replies, "You will not really understand that unless you are caught up out of the ocean someday."

Our society and culture make up an all-encompassing environment in which we live from our birth onward. Countless assumptions, habits of mind, and ways of doing things seem so natural to us that we assume they are the only reality. They infiltrate our faith and spirituality as well.

It has often been noted, for example, that American and European missionaries mixed a great deal of their own culture with the gospel when they took it to foreign lands, and that they often failed to separate what was truly gospel from what was simply a part of their own culture's assumptions. They imposed the whole package of Christianity-and-culture on the native peoples, often to their detriment.

I will never forget an experience I had many years ago in

Africa on a certain Sunday. In the morning I attended a worship service near the compound where I was visiting for a week. The people sat in straight rows on cement benches in a square-walled building under a tin roof. They sweltered in the African heat as they sang European hymns in an off-key, dirge-like manner. It was awful.

But in the evening I was taken to another place of worship several miles away. There I heard drums and lively African singing as I approached an open, thatch-roofed building supported by poles. People either stood or sat on grass mats on the floor. And after a while, these people began to dance to the drumbeats and the joyful singing of songs of salvation in their own words and with their own music. It was wonderful. I had been brought up in a religious tradition that thought dancing was wrong. I could plainly see that this was a culturally conditioned viewpoint that simply didn't apply to African worship!

It usually takes traveling or living in another culture, or having close friendships and intense dialogues with people of other cultures, for us to develop a perspective on our own faith and spirituality that helps us discern the difference between Christ's Gospel and the "gospel" of the society and culture in which we were raised. Even then we have blind spots that need to be pointed out to us by those who were not raised as we were. This is one of the great benefits of the modern ecumenical movement and the multicultural context in which it takes place. To see with the eyes of Christians from other cultures is to have the experience of being "fished out of the ocean" so that we can get a glimpse of our unexamined assumptions.

For instance, as American Christians dialogue with Christians of other cultures more frequently and openly, they discover whole new ways of seeing. They find that South American Christians have a different understanding of freedom in Christ — one that places a greater emphasis on social justice — than do most North Americans, who do not suffer the political oppression that makes the lives of their neighbors to the south so difficult. They also discover that black South African Christians have quite a different interpretation of what Scripture says about how to relate to government than do American Christians, who haven't suffered the cruel oppression of apartheid enforced by the very power that is supposed to insure justice for all, according to Scripture.

A few more general examples will illustrate how American society and Western culture have shaped our faith and spirituality.

We start with the individual and apply the teachings of Scripture in an individual way. But Christians in other cultures often start with the family and "people" (tribe, nation) and apply the teachings of Scripture in a corporate, communal sense. The individualism we take so much for granted is in stark contrast with the emphasis on community and the body of believers that we find in the Bible as well as in many other cultures. For example, there is an enormous difference between seeing salvation as first of all applying to an individual's eternal destiny (heaven or hell) and seeing salvation as first of all applying to the well-being and destiny of a body of people, and only secondarily to individuals because they are part of that body. There is plenty of evidence for both viewpoints in Scripture.

The materialism of our society also profoundly affects us. Millions of American Christians believe that "the good life" must include prosperity. Many preachers proclaim that God wants us all to be rich. In spite of the many warnings against riches and the love of money that are found in Scripture, especially in the New Testament, it is easy to be more influenced by the advertising that bombards us every day with messages which assure us that we will be happy, successful, and/or popular if only we will drive this or that kind of car, buy brand-name clothes, drink a particular sort of beer, and so on. The idea of deliberately choosing a simple lifestyle or of loving "Lady Poverty," as Saint Francis did, goes against our grain — not because these are unbiblical ideas but because they are so foreign to our society.

"Violence is as American as apple pie," said a civil rights leader during the upheaval of the sixties. And he was right. In many ways — despite some of its claims to the contrary — our society approves of violence as a way to achieve one's goals. This assumption, like the others mentioned so far, profoundly influences which Bible passages we heed, which texts we emphasize, which image of God we hold up, and the choices we constantly make in the way we treat others, especially those weaker than ourselves, like children. Many Christians quote biblical texts that allow for capital punishment, the use of force against those who threaten us, and the physical punishment of children ("spare the rod, and spoil the child"), meanwhile paying scant attention to other texts that call for us to love our enemies and welcome children as if they were Christ himself. They choose the texts they do because of the culture they live in, although they may not realize this.

One of the starkest examples of culture-specific readings of Scripture was provided by Christian slaves and Christian slave-owners in earlier centuries. They read and interpreted the Bible, especially the story of the Exodus, in profoundly different ways. Slaves focused on how God freed the Israelite slaves from their Egyptian owners. They felt that Jesus' words "Do unto others as you would have them do unto you" provided more than sufficient grounds to outlaw slavery. Not surprisingly, slave-owners, to justify having slaves, quoted Paul's injunctions to slaves to obey their masters. Owners focused on how the Israelites grumbled and disobeyed and even wanted to go back to Egypt. Clearly, the culture of that time influenced the slave-owners' use of Scripture; the slaves' interpretation went against the culture.

The widespread abuse of women and children in Christian homes as well as in non-Christian homes is another example of the influence of our culture's approval of violence. Verses that tell women to be submissive and children to be obedient are quoted out of context to justify such abuse; verses that contain Jesus' commands to love others in the same way Jesus loves are ignored. Plainly, the violence of our culture and its constant presence in the media subtly incline many Christians toward violence themselves — and, what is worse, the justification of it.

These examples highlight only a few of the many characteristics of American society and culture that influence our attitudes, thoughts, and choices. But how do these characteristics affect the ways in which we are able to receive the spiritual nourishment that God offers us?

What can happen to us in worship provides one obvious example. I experienced this in a vivid way one summer when I spent a week at a religious conference during which African-Americans led worship in their own special style. Those of us white folk

87

who were there joined in the exuberant singing, swaying, and clapping. But when I and the five other people who had attended the conference got back home to our own church, we found that even when we used African-American music, it was really hard for our white congregation to loosen up and get into the feeling and rhythm of African-American worship.

It is also the case that in many parts of our country these days, church attendance is not the norm but the exception. In fact, many Americans view worship as puzzling, irrelevant, old-fashioned, and basically useless. Those who are surrounded by these attitudes will probably find it more difficult to enjoy worship regularly. And if they didn't have regular worship experience when they were growing up, or if their experience was negative, they will find it doubly difficult.

Undoubtedly, our society's emphasis on entertainment, and the omnipresence of television and other media in our homes and all around us, make it difficult for us to take the time to use *lectio divina*. We are constantly bombarded by images that don't last much longer than a fingersnap. All our conditioning tempts us to race through a biblical passage, rather than linger long and lovingly over its words and their meaning.

When it comes to receiving spiritual nourishment from dreams and images, we need lots of encouragement and support, especially in the face of the widespread view in our culture that dreams are not meaningful and that imagining is a waste of time. Even if we can convince ourselves that our imaginations can nurture the welfare of our souls, so much of our imagining has been and is being done for us — especially those of us young enough to have been raised with television — that we may find it difficult to go inward and create our own images.

When we try to find nourishment for our souls in silence, it often feels like we're swimming upstream. Our society is filled with noise and activity, and it is highly suspicious of silence and the desire to be alone. So it takes real effort to shut out the ever-present noise of radios, television, and talk so that we can be still. Moreover, the idea of taking time for "retreat" is simply not honored. Taking activity-filled vacations is fine. Going hunting, fishing, golfing, or boating is fine — but not the sacred leisure of resting in God's presence. It takes great determination to schedule silence and solitude into our lives and enjoy their fruits in the face of misunderstanding and even scorn.

The one kind of spiritual food our cultural conditioning may make more palatable is that of physical spirituality. In our society, sensuous pleasure and the life of the body do receive a great deal of attention, although of a misguided and distorted kind. Nevertheless, when we bring the sacred, spiritual dimension — the vivid sense of the presence of God — into our everyday physical experiences, we can enjoy the Feast in a way that brings meaning into the physical aspects of our lives and bears witness to our culture that our sensuous experience is even better when it is Spirit-filled.

The important thing we need to do as creatures who are inevitably shaped by our culture is to become aware of how we are influenced and how our conditioning makes us prefer some foods over others at the Table. We can also make special efforts to see things as people of other cultures see them — through travel and friendships, for example — and in this way become better at recognizing the unexamined assumptions that make us think and behave as we do. The more aware we are of our assumptions, the better able we are to choose discriminatingly from the foods at the Table.

To me, the Banqueting Table is in some ways like one of those wonderful ethnic food festivals in which one can wander from booth to booth, sampling the marvels of cuisine from every part of the world. I remember going to such a festival with my children when they were young, and being both amused and dismayed because all they wanted to try were the hot dogs and the Dutch baked goods. I, on the other hand, was savoring curried vegetables, Syrian bread, Polish sausage, Irish coffee, and a host of other delicacies. I was so glad that I was free to sample so much and enjoy such a variety of foods because I wasn't limited by fear or ignorance. I liked trying out all the different dishes concocted by the cooks of various cultures. I still think I am the richer and better for it.

If we can come to the Banqueting Table of God with a freedom of spirit, a willingness to experiment, and an awareness of the influence of our own cultural, religious, and family backgrounds that will free us from being so limited by them, the nourishment available to us will be a rich and varied feast for our souls.

✳   ✳   ✳

Here are some specific spiritual exercises to help you further explore the material in this chapter and integrate it into your life:

1. Find a picture of yourself as a little child and enter into an imaginary dialogue or scene or memory with him or her. Ask your little child about his or her religious upbringing and memories, and the feelings that went with them. Write down what you say to each other or do together. If a memory needs healing, bring Jesus or the Holy Spirit or another figure you love and trust into the memory, and let that figure change it into a positive memory with as much vivid detail as you can. Allow yourself to feel the difference. As a way to express your experience further, draw, paint, sing, or dance if you like.

2. Visit the worship services of faith traditions quite different from your own and write down your experience, feelings, and reflections. Ask yourself how you might now come to the Feast if you had worshiped regularly in these other ways.

3. Talk to one or more individuals from a different culture. Ask them about their religious experience and beliefs, their values, and how they might respond to the various spiritual foods at the Feast that are discussed in the first half of this book. Better yet, take the initiative to get together a small group of people from various ethnic backgrounds and have weekly or monthly meetings. Spend several weeks or months getting to know and understand each other in a way that allows you to see your own culture and spirituality with new eyes.

Books for Further Reference

1. *New Eyes for Reading: Biblical and Theological Reflections by Women of the Third World,* edited by John S. Pobee and Barbel Von Wartenberg-Potter
   This is a book of reflections by Third World women on Scripture, church, and society. It yields fresh and moving new insights that help us see how culturally conditioned we First World Christians are.

2. *Habits of the Heart: Individualism and Commitment in American Life* by Robert N. Bellah et al.
   This influential book by a student of American culture and his colleagues probes the heart of individualism and how it affects our lives. These insights are important for understanding ourselves as American Christians in this century.

3. *Suffer the Children* by Janet Pais
   This is a hard-hitting little book that probes the mistreatment of children and the effect of children's experience on their spiritual development. Pais offers a fresh new theology of "God the Child" as a basis for a different way of treating children and the child within each of us.

CHAPTER 7

Shaped by Temperament

One of the most fascinating and frustrating aspects of life is the mystery and even strangeness of other people. They come in such bewildering variety. They act in ways we often find incomprehensible. They are notoriously difficult to figure out or control, although many of us spend a great deal of time and energy trying to do both anyway. Even the people we know best — our spouses, best friends, lovers, parents, sisters and brothers, children, and co-workers — often surprise us.

What is even more disconcerting is to find that we are often mysteries to ourselves. We're not that easy to figure out or control, either. Words pop out of our mouths, thoughts pop into our heads, and actions "happen" that take us by surprise. Just when we think we finally know and understand ourselves, we find ourselves changing! The closer attention we pay to ourselves and the more self-aware we become, the more we realize what strange and mysterious creatures we are.

On the other hand, keen observers of human nature throughout the ages have noticed that there are discernible patterns or types of human temperament and personality, in the same way that there are "body types": short, tall, stocky, slender, big, little. Just as no two people look exactly alike, so no two people have exactly the same temperament. Nevertheless, there are certain generalizations that can be made (cautiously!) about human beings that can help us better understand both ourselves and others.

One of the earliest descriptions of "character types" comes from Greek civilization through Hippocrates. He categorized people into four main types: choleric, phlegmatic, melancholic, and sanguine. These names derive from what were then considered to be the four main body fluids — blood, phlegm, yellow bile, and black bile — and the theories spun around this view lasted through the Middle Ages and into the Renaissance. In fact, this ancient "type" theory has been resurrected recently in evangelical Christian circles and modified for use as a therapeutic tool. However, the arcane and outmoded science behind this theory makes its usefulness limited.

The characteristics of the four temperaments that Hippocrates described are more accessible to us when they are represented by the four gods and goddesses who function as metaphors for the four temperaments.

Apollo and Artemis represent the type of person in whom intuitive functions are the strongest. Apollo is often represented by the sun and Artemis by the moon, both of which are heavenly bodies with a strong symbolic significance.

Athena and Prometheus represent the type of person in whom intellectual functions are the strongest. The owl, representing Athena, and the fire, representing Prometheus, depict aspects of the wisdom and creativeness that these deities symbolize.

Aphrodite, the goddess of love and beauty, and Dionysius, the god of wine, represent the type of person in whom sensuous, earthy functions are the strongest. Things that bring sensory delight — wine and food, flowers and perfumes, beauty of all kinds — are associated with this god and goddess.

Epimetheus and Demeter represent the type of person in whom loyalty and deeply personal values function most strongly. Demeter is often symbolized by the harvested grains and fruits of the earth, which represent the faithful return of seedtime and harvest every year. The story of how she lost and then found her daughter also illustrates her strong loyalty to and love for her child.

The stories about these gods and goddesses are, if we have the eyes to see it, sophisticated and enlightening descriptions of the personality patterns that we can observe being expressed by human beings in a wide variety of cultures, places, and situations.

We might call them "psychological archetypes." Only in the last few decades has the notion that there are such personality patterns once again gained favor in our society.

After the Enlightenment, the traditional way of classifying personality types fell out of favor as ideas that favored individualism and democracy grew in influence. By the twentieth century, there was a widespread notion in the West that people are fundamentally equal — and alike. Sigmund Freud believed that everyone was driven from within by the sexual drive. Alfred Adler saw everyone as driven by the hunger for power. Harry Stack Sullivan claimed that the desire for social solidarity was the basic instinctual drive that defined humans. These and other psychologists and social scientists made claims that were wide-ranging, yet had one thing in common: each asserted that all humans were primarily driven by one instinct.

But beginning in 1920, Freud's younger colleague, Carl Jung, disagreed, producing much evidence and many arguments to support the view that people are different in fundamental ways, even though everyone does have the same instincts or "archetypes" that influence them from within. He claimed that people have different preferences which are inborn, and that these determine how people function. He described the "function types" or "psychological types" in ways that bore strong resemblance to the classical typology described above.

Jung identified the four major functions as those of thinking, feeling, sensing, and intuiting. All people, he said, function in all four ways, but each person prefers and therefore chooses one of these as his or her favorite way of functioning, followed by the others in descending order. How someone functions in his or her preferred ways is also influenced by his or her perceptions or judgments and whether he or she is extroverted or introverted.

A great deal of what Jung said was unclear, complicated, and undeveloped. By the 1950s, his theory was largely ignored in favor of "behaviorist" or "dynamic" psychologies, until two women, Isabel Myers and her mother, Katheryn Briggs, devised the Myers-Briggs Type indicator. This personality test became so widely used that it sparked a renewed interest in temperament theory which is still strong today. The book *Please Understand Me* by David

Keirsey and Marilyn Bates provides more information about temperament theory: it offers a helpful description of various personality types and how these types function in work settings, in marriage, and so on.

Of course, there are other ways of describing people according to temperament and personality, and each has its own usefulness for helping us understand how our particular type influences the way we approach and feast at the Banqueting Table, and why certain foods are more appealing to us than others.

A description that I have found helpful, because it deals directly with the spiritual aspects and consequences of personality and temperament type, is found in the book *Prayer and Temperament* by Chester Michael and Marie Norrisey. The authors make several fascinating suggestions about the various kinds of temperament reflected in the four Gospels and the epistles of Paul, Peter, John, and James. Jesus Christ, the authors say, is clearly *the* truly whole human being who functions fully in all the ways described by personality theory. In defining the basic temperaments, the authors rely on the personality types described in *Please Understand Me* and then correlate them with the types of spiritual temperaments exemplified by four great spiritual leaders in the Christian tradition: Saint Augustine, Saint Aquinas, Saint Francis, and Saint Ignatius. I am indebted to Michael and Norrisey for the following descriptions of the four basic temperaments, which are drawn from their work.

The Augustinian temperament is strongly intuitive. If this is your type, you tend to see and know more from your intuition, sixth sense, inner eye, and hunches than you do from your five physical senses. You are the sort of person, for example, who can walk into a roomful of people and just sense that something is wrong. You have a way of feeling what is invisible, under the surface, less than obvious.

You are more interested in the future than in the past or the present. You are more likely to be wondering about what lies ahead than taking careful note of your current circumstances. You prefer to think of the possibilities in people and situations. This makes you a natural visionary, able to inspire others with your ability to envision the future.

Your intuitive ability makes it easy for you to see meaning in everything, and symbolic thinking is your forte. You probably like poetry and relate well to metaphor in literature and art. You seldom take things literally or at face value, and you love to use your imagination. Dreams and visions probably fascinate you, and you prefer fiction and fantasy to newspapers and how-to manuals.

Your choices are based more on the values important to you, and your deeply held convictions and strongly felt beliefs, than on logic. You prefer the compassionate rather than the just or logical approach, and your heart leads more often than your head. You probably have a warm and empathetic personality, and relate well to the feelings and values of others because your own are important to you.

It is likely that you thrive on change and challenge, and would rather start something than maintain it over the long haul. It isn't easy for you to concentrate on the details of day-to-day management because you're usually thinking of what is ahead rather than paying close attention to what is at hand.

Chances are you communicate well and can be persuasive and insightful. You are probably good with words and enjoy writing, especially creative, imaginative writing. In fact, it could be that you, like Saint Augustine, "pray at the point of a pen."

If you identify with the Augustinian type, you will find yourself in the company of many visionary prophets like Daniel and Isaiah, poets like William Blake and Emily Dickinson, and artists like Leonardo da Vinci and Georgia O'Keefe. Some folks think that Saint John is clearly an Augustinian type. His emphasis on love in his epistles and his visions in the book of Revelation certainly seem to support this view. In short, you're in good company!

The Thomistic type of temperament, whose paradigm is Thomas Aquinas, is also intuitive, but even more strongly characterized by the thinking function. If you are of this type, you are mildly interested in the future, but you are really most comfortable outside the realm of time in the realm of ideas.

You love thinking, logic, and reason, and through them you come to know the truth about the world. You are investigative and curious, and you love ideas, which makes you a genuine intellectual, even if you don't have an advanced academic degree. You think things through, and you probably don't follow your hunches very often because you trust the thinking process as the best way to arrive at what is true and real.

Because thinking is so important to you, it is harder for you to be in touch with your feelings, and you often seem impersonal to others. You relate much better to them on a thinking level than on a feeling level. You probably love stimulating intellectual discussions and shun small talk and "touchy-feely" groups. Your head usually leads over your heart, and you prefer taking the just, rational approach over basing your decisions on feelings or values.

As a Thomistic type, you need to make sense of faith and life. Coherence is important to you, and you are not afraid to ask lots of questions and follow them wherever they take you, because you want to know the truth. You probably aren't content with easy answers and want very much to be right in your conclusions. You may be prone to perfectionism, which makes you quite demanding of both yourself and others and intolerant of what seems stupid or irrational to you.

Chances are you like structure, setting goals and making step-by-step plans for achieving them, and leading your life, including your spiritual life, in an orderly manner. You are seldom impulsive or spontaneous; you prefer to think things through before you speak and act.

In your relationships with people, you tend to be straightforward, clear, and logical. Sometimes you come across as impersonal and terse, because you don't like to beat around the bush or say more than you need to for the purpose at hand.

If you recognize yourself in this description, you will find yourself in the company of theologians, mathematicians, scientists, philosophers, and the like. John Calvin, Leibniz, Madame Curie, and Immanuel Kant are all people of your type. Some people think that Saint Matthew and Saint Paul tended toward the Thomistic temperament because their writings reflect Thomistic attention to structure, logic, and argument. Again, you're in good company!

In contrast with the two intuitive kinds of temperaments just described, the Franciscan temperament relies strongly on the senses. If you are of this type, you are most interested in the here and now rather than the past or the future. You're good at living in the moment, and this makes you a desirable person to have around during crisis, which you handle well. You probably don't like long-term planning or appeals to tradition, but prefer being spontaneous and "going with the flow." You're a flexible person and a good troubleshooter. You might even be impulsive fairly often.

You apprehend things primarily through your five senses. You are oriented toward the concrete and the physical rather than dreams and visions. You notice details, and things are what they are; they don't mean something else. Poetry, fantasy, and metaphorical thinking are not your forte. You tend to take things literally.

Saint Francis was a literalist, as the story of his famous vision illustrates. He was praying in a ruined, deserted church outside his hometown of Assisi in Italy when he heard the voice of the Lord saying, "Francis, rebuild My Church." Saint Francis took this to literally mean he was supposed to rebuild the broken-down church in which he was praying. So he proceeded to enlist the help of others, mostly the poor, in building it up stone by stone. Of course, as it turns out, what God had in mind was the church as the family of God. But Saint Francis did build up God's spiritual church in his lifetime, and he left a legacy of followers through which his work has continued.

If you are like Saint Francis in temperament, you don't want rules and structure; you much prefer trying new things. Adventure, challenge, drama, and excitement are appealing to you, and your optimistic outlook on life helps you enjoy them all. You tend to see God's beauty and loving care in creation, and you feel especially close to God in nature. You have a strong aesthetic sense, and you might have great artistic ability.

Praise comes naturally to you, and you pray best through your senses, while going about the business of your daily life. You prefer to serve others with concrete, physical action, and you have a strong practical bent. You notice the physical needs of others, and you know how to meet those needs.

If you recognize yourself in this description, you will find yourself in the company of such people as Florence Nightingale,

Harriet Tubman, and perhaps the Apostle Peter and Saint Luke. Certainly the latter two individuals seemed very much in touch with their senses, and Peter was such a literalist that the voice which spoke to him in the vision he had on the rooftop of Simon the Tanner's house had to explain to him that "unclean" referred not only in a literal way to the animals in the sheet that he saw lowered from heaven, but also to Gentiles, who were called "unclean" by Jews. In the Gospel stories, Peter is also impulsive and a man of concrete action. Clearly, you're in good company!

The individual with an Ignatian temperament, who relies strongly on both thought and the senses, takes a very practical approach to life. If you fit this type, you are a person with a strong sense of history and a respect for tradition. You value continuity and are probably fairly conservative, albeit in a thoughtful way. You appreciate time-honored ceremonies and rituals, and you and those like you are the preservers and stabilizers in society.

You use your physical senses as well as common sense to reach your conclusions, but you do so in a much more structured and deliberate manner than Franciscan types. You learn through the concrete and visible, and you're good at paying attention to detail. You're a good manager and would probably be a good administrator. You tend to do hands-on work effectively as well, and you probably have a strong work ethic. In all likelihood you are conscientious, thorough, and responsible, and you find it hard to turn down requests for things that need doing. Not surprisingly, you therefore find yourself overworked quite often.

You're not fond of change — you usually prefer the status quo — and you don't like surprises very much, either. You prefer the tried and true. For example, you might especially treasure the liturgical year, with its appeal to tradition, repetition, and the senses through such time-honored symbols as the Advent wreath, the cross, the liturgical colors, and so on. Your preferences make it hard for you to be very flexible, and you're much more comfortable with the predictable and with dependable structure.

Because your thinking function is strong, you're probably not very much in touch with your feelings or those of others. It's hard for you to feel deeply with people or sense how you may be affecting them. You would rather be "in your head," figuring yourself out or figuring them out, because it's hard for you to intuit the right way to relate to them. On the other hand, you are very helpful in a practical, no-nonsense way, and concrete action is your forte, especially if you can plan the action in advance.

You tend to be pessimistic rather than optimistic, and it's a challenge for you to be trusting and hopeful, especially because you're so aware of the past and all the ways the human race has failed and fallen. The majority of church members are like you, which is one of the reasons the institutional church has survived as long and as well as it has, from a human point of view!

If you identify with the Ignatian temperament, you are in the company of such people as Oliver Cromwell, Edward Pusey, and other leaders of the Oxford Movement in the Anglican Church, and perhaps the Apostle James and Saint Mark, both of whom exhibit in their writings a remarkable practicality and an approach that is both action-oriented and sense-oriented. Again, you're in good company!

These four temperaments more or less describe us all in one way or another, and give us some important information about ourselves as feasters at the Banqueting Table. If you have some sense of which type you are, keep it in mind and try it on for size and "feel" as you read the ways in which different types can find nourishment at the Feast.

Worship

If you are Augustinian in type, you especially appreciate symbols in worship and metaphorical or poetic preaching. The sacraments have a special meaning to you as symbolic conveyors of deep spiritual truth. You probably like variety and change in worship and enjoy appeals to your heart. You value a sense of warmth, caring, and emotional engagement in worship, but you also need and appreciate a preacher who is a good communicator. In fact, many people of your type *are* pastors and preachers and thus are able to implement the things they value in worship.

If you are Thomistic in type, you really appreciate good doctrinal sermons that are logical, clear, and thoughtful. You like

COME TO THE FEAST

a well-ordered worship service, and you may be uncomfortable with emotional appeals or too much "coziness." You don't need to have warm, close contact with others in worship, and if you get into conversations afterward, they are probably intellectual discussions of ideas. You often have questions about the sermon or church teachings, and you appreciate opportunities to explore them.

If you are Franciscan in type, you love worship that appeals to your physical senses and your feelings. Doctrinal sermons often seem dry to you, and logical explorations of biblical truth don't excite you. You also love a sacramental approach because it involves concreteness and appeal to the senses: the light of candles, the scent of Easter lilies, the wine and bread of communion, the water of baptism. You may be quite open to charismatic experience in worship, and you don't need a lot of structure and sameness. Worship that allows for considerable flexibility and spontaneity pleases you. You like drama in worship too, and lots of praise.

If you are Ignatian in type, you treasure a structured, dependable, traditional worship service with which you are familiar and comfortable, and which gives you a strong sense of continuity with the past. You appreciate a service that is well-planned and organized, and you're uncomfortable with spontaneity and improvisation. Like the Thomistic type, you don't respond well to emotional appeals, and you don't need warm, emotional contact with fellow worshipers in any regular way. You appreciate sermons that are practical and concrete. Sitting around talking about ideas is not your preference; instead, you enjoy opportunities for action and service with others.

Lectio: *Divine Reading*

Actually, all four temperaments find *lectio* valuable, but in different ways. Augustinian types will read Scripture as if it were speaking directly to their hearts, like a love letter from God. If you are of this type, you will find it easy to apply its meaning to your life in a personal way. You will get the most out of Scripture passages that allow you to use your intuitions and feelings, such as the

Psalms, the prophets, Jesus' parables, and Revelation. When you meditate upon Scripture, you'll enjoy using your imagination and seeing how it might shed light on the future. For you, the heartfelt prayer of response that is the third step will usually be quite natural and easy, as will resting in silence in the presence of God.

If you have the Thomistic type of temperament, you will feel right at home in the rational, methodical Bible-study approach that is common in the Protestant tradition. You will also enjoy pursuing a line of reasoning in response to the Scripture you have read and exploring its ideas in a logical manner. The doctrinal passages in Paul's letters will probably have a special appeal for you. You will find that your prayer grows more out of your intellect than your emotion. You may feel drawn to setting specific goals for yourself as part of your response to the Scripture you read. It is probably difficult for you to quiet your busy mind in order to enjoy the silence of the fourth step.

If you most identify with the Franciscan personality type, you will find that *lectio* needs to involve your feelings and your senses to be most fruitful. Those Scripture passages that are most vivid and descriptive and that involve both feelings and the senses, like the Psalms and stories, will have great appeal to you, as will the portions that offer instruction in specific, concrete action as an expression of faith. Your meditation and prayer will be best when you can use music or movement or paint or clay or flowers — concrete things — in your response. The place where you do *lectio* will help you greatly if it has things in it that support your prayer visually — an open Bible, a candle, incense, a sacred picture, flowers, and so on. You will probably want to change the objects you use so that you have a variety over time. You may also find that praying out in nature works wonders for you, and that *lectio* for you can expand beyond reading words on a printed page to listening to God's message through a tree, a bird's song, or a star-filled sky. You may find it hard to sit still during the last step of *lectio*, and you will find it helpful to put your response to God's Word into concrete actions of service to others as soon as possible.

If you have an Ignatian temperament, *lectio* will be most satisfying for you when you are able to put yourself into a parable or story by using your senses and a structured method for doing so, like that suggested by the *Spiritual Exercises* of St. Ignatius. You will especially enjoy such commonsense and practical Scriptures as the books of Proverbs and James, and you will probably want to plan action in response to them as part of your meditation and prayer. Because you tend to be pessimistic by nature, you will find especially important those passages that encourage you to trust and hope. Because of your strong appreciation for history, you will get a great deal out of the historical books of the Bible as well as other books of church history, stories of the lives of the saints, and so on. For you too, the silence at the end of *lectio* will not be easy unless you can fill it with vivid images that you "live into" with your five senses. But if you can rest in an image rather than being overeager to move on to concrete implementation, it will aid your effort to be quiet in God's presence.

Silence

If you are Augustinian in type, it is likely that you will be more able than any other type of person to fold the wings of your intellect and rest in your heart. With the aid of your imagination, you can quietly enjoy God's presence in silence and solitude. In fact, your type needs silence and time alone with God more than most, and when you don't get it, you tend to quickly become tense and out of sorts.

If you are Thomistic in type, you will enjoy silence if you can use it for quiet reflection and thought. Solitude is an important part of helping you develop your thinking capacity, and you will probably enjoy the freedom from interruptions that it affords. However, your mind is probably occupied and busy, and you will find it hard to become still and silent within.

If you are Franciscan in type, you will need to give yourself the freedom to use your senses during silence, and then it will be fruitful and wonderful for you. Listening to meditative music, singing songs of praise, playing instruments in a prayerful way, drawing and painting, playing with clay, wandering alone in silence in a meadow or along the beach — all these are ways in which you are particularly able to enjoy silence and solitude. You will need to use your silence in an unstructured, spontaneous, and free-flowing manner. If you try to plan what you will do, you might become frustrated. You need permission to enjoy silence and solitude playfully!

If you are Ignatian in type, you will enjoy silence and solitude best in a structured way, perhaps at a retreat center in a directed retreat that allows you to have long periods of silence but also offers you regular opportunity to talk with a retreat director who is familiar with Ignatian-type spiritual exercises, so that you can reflect upon what is happening for you in the silence. You will flourish if you can schedule these retreats regularly and dependably into your calendar, and if you read about the experience and uses of silence by spiritual leaders in the past, so that you will be solidly rooted in tradition.

Physical Spirituality

If you identify with the Augustinian temperament, you will find this kind of spiritual nourishment rather difficult, because your strengths do not lie in either using your senses or using your imagination. You are more comfortable with your intuition, imagination, and feelings. You will need special energy and support in order to really focus on the present moment rather than wandering off into the future, which is your natural inclination. When you take a walk, for instance, you will need to make a special effort to tune in to your senses, to be aware of your physical surroundings. Painting, drawing, playing with clay, and the like are not natural and easy for you, but they will sharpen your ability to use your senses and become more comfortable with a sensuous spirituality.

If you identify with the Thomistic temperament, you will also find physical spirituality difficult. In fact, it will be even harder for you than for Augustinian types, because your strengths do not lie in either using your senses or using your imagination. Not only is it hard for you to be truly in your body, in your feelings, in the present moment; you also have that busy, thinking mind of yours pulling you away from your senses and into your head. It will be tempting for you to simply dismiss the physical way of spiritual nourishment, but if you can pause long enough now and then to savor the pleasure of your senses each day, even if only for a few moments — while you're in the shower, or taking a walk, or eating dinner — you will find it a powerful means of restoring your soul and making you more whole.

If you identify with the Franciscan temperament, physical spirituality probably nourishes you more than anything else at the Banqueting Table. Using your senses is your forte, and praying with your senses is what you naturally want to do most of the time. Nothing appeals to you more than using your body as a way of praying, and for you it is wonderfully rewarding to pray through the day with your senses. You find it easy to pray through both physical work and play, and because this is so, you are able to have a lively sense of the presence of God throughout each day.

If you identify with the Ignatian temperament, you will also find it quite easy to enjoy sensuous prayer, because using your senses is also a strength for you. However, you will enjoy planning how and when you enjoy the physical way of being spiritual, rather than "going with the flow" as Franciscan types do. You will also enjoy what fits most comfortably into your own religious tradition, and that will affect how much experimentation you do. If you are Catholic or Orthodox, you will enjoy incense far more than if you are Baptist or Presbyterian. You will also enjoy your sensory experience in a practical way; because of your strong work ethic and sense of responsibility, you probably would rather weave sensuous prayer into your everyday work than take special time out for it. If you have a good idea of how physical spirituality is part of the Christian tradition and how it has been practiced by Christians in the past, you will also feel better about trying it, especially if it is a fairly new approach for you.

Dreams and Visions

If you are Augustinian in type, dreams and visions are a natural and easy way for you to meditate and pray, and they nourish your soul. Your strong intuitive ability enables you to see the meaning in the metaphors and symbols that are the stuff of dreams and visions. Your natural inclination to look to the future and to see "behind the scenes" makes you open to messages from the Holy Spirit through dreams and visions that other types are not as able to receive. Your passionate beliefs and ability to communicate well enable you to share what you see in a way that can be helpful — and challenging — to others.

If you are Thomistic in type, you will be able to receive nourishment from your dreams and visions because of your intuitive ability, but you will tend to focus on thinking about them and figuring them out in an orderly way. Your need to make sense of things and your valuing of the rational will raise many questions for you as you ponder your dreams and visions. You will tend to experience more frustration with them than Augustinian types do because of your need to be logical — which dreams and visions are not! It is important for you to find a method for discerning their meaning that makes sense to you and satisfies you.

If you are Franciscan in type, you will find it rather difficult to get nourishment from dreams and visions. Your intuition is your weakest faculty, and because you tend to take things literally and have a hard time thinking symbolically, you will also have a hard time discerning the meaning of dreams and visions. They usually won't make sense to you unless you can take them literally. Since dreams and visions occur in the inner rather than in the outer world, they don't seem real or very important to you. But if you can use your senses when you ponder dreams or visions, you will at least be able to get some nourishment from them, even if you can't get at their meaning symbolically. Wise and experienced Augustinian types can be helpful companions for you at the Feast if you share your dreams and visions with them.

If you are Ignatian in type, you will be able to get the most out of your dreams and visions by using your imagination in a methodical way — by entering into familiar scenes from Scripture, for example. You will get nourishment from reflecting on such experiences in a more sense-centered, literal way, rather than trying to extract their symbolic meaning as Augustinian types do. Because you need to be rational and structured in your approach and because practicality and common sense are very important to you,

you will probably find it difficult to get much nourishment from your dreams. You will probably do much better if you undertake guided meditations as a way of enjoying nourishing visions.

❋   ❋   ❋

As the preceding explanations indicate, knowing which temperament best describes who you are at this stage in your life is important if you are to discern how best to be nourished by the Feast. However, there are four other personality traits that are also important to consider as you try to discern what foods at the Banqueting Table are best for you and how to feast upon them in the most appropriate way.

The first trait is extroversion. If you are an extrovert, you are a person who is usually energized by being with people and by lots of stimulation in your environment. You find out what you think and feel by talking with other people and by processing things out loud. Even though you need and even enjoy some time alone, you are not naturally contemplative; you are basically a people person. How does this affect what foods at the Feast best nourish you?

As an extrovert, you prefer worship that provides lots of stimulation and plenty of activity. When it comes to *lectio,* you do better if you can process the meaning of what you have read out loud with at least one other person. You are likely to enjoy good discussion groups for this reason. Silence and solitude can be difficult for you because they involve your processing your thoughts and feelings alone. If you go on a retreat, you would be better off having someone there whom you can talk with from time to time, so you can process what is happening inside you. Because physical spirituality has to do with communing with God through your senses with things in the outside world, you will be able to find real nourishment in this way, even if you are Augustinian in type. You will get the greatest benefit from working with dreams and visions if you can process them with someone else, because these are inner happenings, and you are more geared toward what happens outside of yourself.

The second trait is introversion. If you are an introvert, you need to spend a lot more time alone than an extrovert does in order to process all the activity that is constantly going on inside you. Being with people, especially in groups, often drains you, and parties are usually not appealing to you. If there is a lot of stimulating activity going on around you, it bothers you, because as an introvert you already have so much going on inside you. You much prefer processing your responses within, and you usually have to ponder a while before you can say what you really think or feel. You are more contemplative by nature, and you enjoy being alone. How does this trait affect what foods at the Feast best nourish you?

Worship that is contemplative, that includes ample time for silence and reflection, and that isn't too wordy or active is what nourishes you most. As for *lectio,* you prefer plenty of time to process the Word by yourself, in silence. Silence is just what you need, and its fruits are a delight to you. If you are in a discussion group, you are less likely to speak up. You don't need much guidance or need to spend much time processing things with others, and you find directed retreats less appealing than solitary ones. Sensuous prayer is more difficult for you, because it involves your relating more to what is outside of you than what is inside. It is a more extroverted way to pray. But if you can do it slowly, by yourself, in silence, you can find real nourishment through sensuous prayer too. You might find that processing responses to the prayer in some physical way that involves solitary activity — through art or dance or music — is more helpful to you than processing things by talking with someone else. Dreams and visions will probably appeal to you because they are inner events, and you are basically most attracted to what is going on inside you. Working with them in ways that allow you plenty of time for reflection in solitude will make them truly nourishing for your soul.

The third and fourth personality traits have to do with whether you are a decisive person or a spontaneous person. The decisive person prefers structure and planning and likes to come to closure quickly. The spontaneous person doesn't like making decisions until all the information is in, likes to keep things open-ended, and prefers to go with the flow and live more moment to moment.

If you are a decisive person who prefers structure, you will like worship that is structured and well planned. You will want a definite method that takes you through *lectio* step by step. You will tend to plan ways to use your time for solitude and silence. You will probably even prefer to figure out when and how best to pray with your senses. And when you work with dreams and visions, you will want a good method for doing so, and you will need to come to some conclusions about their meaning, and how to act on that meaning, as soon as possible.

On the other hand, if you are a more spontaneous person who dislikes a lot of structure and planning and likes to keep things open-ended, you will get more from worship that allows for spontaneous engagement and that is flexible in format. You will want to do *lectio* in an experimental, go-with-the-flow way, perhaps concentrating on different aspects of the steps at different times. When you take time out for silence and solitude, you will do best if you give yourself permission to plan very little and just do what your heart leads you to do, hour by hour. When you try sensory prayer, you will also find it easiest to be spontaneous about it. You will probably prefer to ponder dreams and visions for quite a while before you come to any definitive conclusions about their meaning or about what action you need to take in response to their messages.

While it is important to be aware of how your temperament type and personality traits influence the way you come to the Banqueting Table, it is also important to remember that putting yourself or others in boxes is not helpful. As each of us goes through life, the goal is to become more balanced and whole. So when you start coming to the Table, it is best to begin by choosing the kinds of sustenance that are most naturally nourishing and appealing for you. But over time, it's best if you sample everything on the Table, even the foods to which you are less suited, because that is what develops your less preferred and therefore less developed capacities.

All of us have the God-given potential to enjoy all the nourishment at the Feast, if we will only be willing to experiment once in a while. The kind of spiritual nourishment that best suits our temperament and our personality will be our mainstay. But we can try other kinds now and then, when we have extra energy and time. In fact, many people have found that they have the most vivid, transforming experiences of communion with God when they are praying out of their weakness. So, for example, those for whom the sensory function is weakest will often find that sensory prayer is what helps them experience God's presence most wonderfully.

This is most likely to happen in the second half of life, when it is especially important for us to develop our unused potential and to reach a balance in our spirituality as well. The impetus to do so is often provided by what we call the "midlife crisis" in our culture. If at this point we cling to old ways and resist change and growth, we can easily turn into brittle old people who have lost their love of life and are one-sided and close-minded. There are enough such people in the world already!

The most important thing to keep in mind is that though each of us may fit certain patterns of personality and temperament, each one of us is a unique individual who is unpredictable in many ways. As long as the descriptions in this chapter (and anywhere else you find them) function as guidelines for self-understanding rather than closed boxes of self-definition or tools for analyzing and pigeonholing other people, they can be helpful. No one fits any single pattern or description exactly, and the more whole we become, the more we become people who defy schemes of analysis and definition. Jesus, the most whole and holy human being who ever lived, certainly does. And we are all called to become more and more completely the image of God that Christ reveals, each of us in her or his own unique way.

❀   ❀   ❀

The following are some spiritual exercises that you can use if you would like to try ways of praying that are particularly suited to the four types of temperament described in this chapter. Try doing all four kinds of exercises as a way of both discerning your own

111

temperament and finding out where your strengths and weaknesses lie. When you try each exercise, write down your experience in your journal. What did the experience of various kinds of prayer teach you about yourself? Did you find the kind of prayer that best suits your temperament? Which way of prayer most nourished your soul? In which way did you most vividly experience God's presence or message for you? I found a number of good examples in *Prayer and Temperament,* four of which I repeat below.[1]

1. Augustinian Prayer Exercise: Read Isaiah 43:1-5

   "Change the words 'Jacob' and 'Israel' to your own first name. Try to imagine [God] speaking these words directly to you. What meaning would they have for you in your present situation? Try to transpose the message from God to yourself today. What is [God] talking about [in the words] 'Fear not'? What fears do you have? . . . What are the greatest dangers you face in your life? What is [God] telling you to do in time of danger? Imagine Jesus saying to you now, 'You are precious in my eyes, and I love you. Fear not, I am with you.' How do you see this to be true in your own situation today?" (p. 65).

2. Thomistic Prayer Exercise: [Read Matt. 18:1-5]

   "Spiritual Childhood: . . .What does Jesus mean when he says that we must become as little children if we wish to enter the Kingdom of Heaven? What are the qualities of a small child that are especially needed in our relationship with God? [with others? with ourselves?] Which of these qualities do you need to intensify and develop at the present time in your life?" (pp. 86-87).

3. Franciscan Prayer Exercise:

   "Watch a beautiful sunset or sunrise. Contemplate the waves of the ocean, a mountain lake, a waterfall, a tree, a leaf, a bee, a beetle, an animal. . . . As you contemplate God's

1. Chester P. Michael and Marie C. Norrisey, *Prayer and Temperament: Different Prayer Forms for Different Personality Types* (Charlottesville, Va.: Open Door, Inc., 1984).

creation, try to come to a better appreciation of God's beauty, power, goodness, love, wisdom" (p. 77).

To this I add my own suggestion: Read Psalm 104 as an inspiration for your own psalm of praise for creation and your experience of it.

4. Ignatian Prayer Exercise: Read Luke 10:38-42
   "Imagine yourself a friend and fellow-villager of either Mary, or Martha, or Lazarus. You happen to meet one of them in the village and you are told that Jesus of Nazareth is coming to visit in Bethany. You express an interest in meeting him, and you are invited to come the next evening to have dinner with them and Jesus. Close your eyes and try to relive in your imagination, with as many vivid details as you can, what your meeting and the ensuing conversation with Jesus would be like. Draw some practical fruit from it" (p. 53).

Books for Further Reference

1. *Prayer and Temperament: Different Prayer Forms for Different Personality Types* by Chester P. Michael and Marie C. Norrisey
   The descriptions of the four classic Christian spiritual temperaments that I have used in this chapter are drawn from this book. It describes these four temperaments in great detail, and also offers many helpful exercises and questions.

2. *Please Understand Me: Character and Temperament Types* by David Kiersey and Marilyn Bates
   This basic book on human personality and temperament gives the reader all kinds of helpful ways to discover his or her own temperament, and explains how various types interact with each other in marriage, work, and religious settings. This is one of the clearest and most helpful guides to the subject available on the market today.

3. *From Image to Likeness: A Jungian Path in the Gospel Journey* by Harold Grant et al.
   This is a thoughtful theological and biblical approach that integrates ideas for living the Gospel with theories about temperament and adult development. A strong Christian perspective provides a good basis for seeing how the spiritual and the psychological are connected.

CHAPTER 8

Affected by Age and Stage

It seems almost too obvious to say: Our age and stage in life have an enormous impact on the kind of spiritual nourishment that is best for us. Nevertheless, it needs saying, because only recently have the psychological and spiritual stages of human development received the kind of attention that helps us discern what sort of nourishment is best for us at any given time.

Children, for example, will relate to those things we discussed in the first part of the book — the church's worship and prayer, the Scriptures, physical spirituality, silence, and dreams and visions — in ways quite different from the ways adults will. The development of Sunday school and "Children in Worship" programs and the composition of Bible-story books and other materials just for children are responses to this fact. In typical Protestant settings, the ability that children have to enter into silence and to use their imaginations has yet to be adequately explored, and encouraging children to use their senses as a way to commune with God depends on the further growth of adults in this area. Nevertheless, many of the discoveries of those who study childhood development have contributed positively to the ways in which children are spiritually nurtured at home and in the church.

Similarly, there has recently been a great deal of investigation into the unique needs of adolescents and the ways in which to best nurture their spiritual development. Again, in Protestant settings there is room for a great deal of exploration of the ways in which teenagers can be nurtured by worship, *lectio,* physical spirituality, silence, and dreams and visions. It is likely that such exploration will reveal that young people do not respond particularly well when they simply ape the approach of adults, just as they seldom respond well when they are treated or "fed" as if they were still children, as in the old "memorizing the catechism" method.

Until recently, it was assumed that once individuals reached adulthood, they did not progress through any further identifiable stages of spiritual development. But the findings of students of adult development have revealed that adults do go through definite stages, both psychologically and spiritually, that need to be understood if they are to receive the right nourishment at the right time in their lives.

Besides these modern discoveries about the unique character of each age and stage of human life, there is much ancient wisdom in Scripture relating to the spiritual-development needs of Christians of all ages. It would be a good idea for us to take a brief look at some of this wisdom, so that it can function as a foundation for further consideration of the effects of age and stage on the way we take in spiritual nourishment.

Several passages in the Epistles, for example, use the metaphors of "milk" and "meat" to distinguish between the kind of nourishment needed by "infants in Christ" and the kind needed by the "mature." In these passages (1 Cor. 2:6, 3:2, 13:9-12; Eph. 4:11-16; Heb. 5:11-14), Christians who are jealous and quarrelsome, who are blown about by various teachings and trends, who have narrow perspectives, who simply swallow the wisdom of "this age," or who have trouble distinguishing between what is truly good and truly evil are all called "children" who need the "milk" of basics.

On the other hand, the "mature" — that is, those who are able to love, forebear, forgive, and understand others; who appreciate the wisdom of God, which is so different from society's wisdom; who are able to distinguish between good and evil and *do* what is good; and who have the broad, full perspective of real maturity — these are ready for the "meat" of more subtle and demanding spiritual teaching or nourishment.

The spiritual development of Christians is described as a

growing consciousness of unity in faith with all others, whatever the differences, and increasing Christ-likeness. Speaking the truth honestly and in love is a principal means of engendering this spiritual growth, along with using one's gifts for the building up of others and the community (Eph. 4). This means that the main mark of Christianity is the increasing freedom and ability to love. It is both God's gift and each individual's responsibility.

An illuminating paradigm is found in the Gospel's description of the spiritual development of Jesus Christ, which is a model for our development as well. By examining Jesus' experiences, we can discern the basic elements of that development.

When Jesus was a baby, he was brought to the temple by his parents to be presented to God. There he was recognized as the Promised One by Simeon and Anna (Luke 2:22-38). Jesus began, as we all do, in the passive state, in which one's spiritual development is dependent on parents and religious community. These are the "givens" that provided Jesus' spiritual nurture, and that provide ours when we are little children. (Some people, unfortunately, grow up with neither, which makes their development all the more difficult.)

I wonder what our childhood experience would have been like if our parents and respected, elderly religious figures like Simeon and Anna had seen us in the same special way that Jesus was seen? What if our unique unfolding and vocation had been seen in all its mystery and meaning and possibility? In any case, Jesus was given the great gift of parents and wise older adults who saw his unique potential and purpose.

But the time came when Jesus had to claim his potential and purpose for himself in his own way. This happened when he was taken to the temple when he was twelve (Luke 2:41-51). At this point he began the process of exploring his own unique relationship with God — of going beyond that which he had been given by his parents and his upbringing. This involved a long and intense time of listening to and asking questions of the wisest people he could find. The result was that Jesus discovered himself to be God's beloved son who "must be about my Father's business." Although he continued to lovingly obey his parents, from that time onward his primary allegiance shifted to God, to his own personal relationship with God, and to what that would mean for his life.

For us, spiritual development means developing this same kind of increasing spiritual autonomy. It involves our asking many questions of wise people, as Jesus did, as well as arriving at our own answers, rather than unthinkingly accepting those that were given to us in our childhood. If we are allowed to do this in the context of a stable, loving religious environment, we too will grow, as Jesus did, "in wisdom and stature and favor with God and others" (Luke 2:52).

Then came the turning point at which Jesus left private, ordinary life to begin his public ministry. After having his identity publicly acknowledged and personally confirmed by God through his baptism, and after identifying himself with Israel and with all of humanity at the same time, Jesus was driven into the wilderness by the Spirit to be tested (Luke 4:1-13). Here his identity as God's chosen and beloved was called into question. He was faced with the dark possibilities of human nature.

We too need to endure a testing process that will help us stand firm in the identity given to us through our baptism as God's beloved. During this process we must recognize the dark possibilities and shadow side of our own lives and beings. This stage in spiritual maturation is necessary, because it can give us an elemental confidence in God's love and purpose for us, and a proper sense of humility as we become conscious of our limits and our potential for doing evil.

As part of his time of trial, Jesus also had a visionary experience in the temple. The devil tempted him to jump from its pinnacle. Whatever else this temptation meant, it most certainly was a temptation to use religion and relationship to God for his own ends — for recognition (think of the amazement of the crowds when he jumped safely to the ground!) and for security ("the angels will bear you up," the devil coaxed). But Jesus firmly rejected this temptation, for he knew that to try to use God for one's own ends is to put God on trial, and that is wrong and dangerous.

This is an important stage in our spiritual development as well. All of us are tempted in some fashion — especially when we embark upon some kind of ministry to others — to use our gifts and position for our own ends. We all want and need recognition and security, of course, so it is tempting for us to use religious life

— our service "in the temple" — to get these things for ourselves rather than serving God's larger purposes. If we succumb to the temptation, we are likely to get "stuck" in our religious development, just as many of the scribes and Pharisees did. Like them and all too many religious leaders of our own day, we will labor under the illusion that we are serving God's purposes by serving "the church," when in reality we are serving only ourselves. We would do well to avoid this trap, as Jesus did.

After his trial in the wilderness, Jesus began preaching and teaching in the synagogues. When he started in Nazareth among the folks with whom he grew up, he demonstrated the next stage of spiritual growth — that of integrating one's beliefs with one's practice and with God's saving purposes for others. Like the prophets in whose footsteps he followed, Jesus saw his vocation in the context of God's call to all people to live a life of justice, integrity, and mercy. He was not willing to let those who thought they knew him so well tell him who he was and what he should do (Luke 4:14-44). He was very clear about what he had discovered his mission to be, and what he would and would not do. This proved to be an unpopular thing, and Jesus barely escaped with his life.

While we may not have to take as great a risk as he did, each of us will also develop spiritually by becoming "God's own person" — by not allowing the opinions of parents, spouses, children, neighbors, or others to overcome our own sense of mission and call. We will follow God's will for our lives, and we will not allow our community or society to deflect us from the unique unfolding and use of our gifts in the context of God's great compassion and desire for justice and healing, especially for the poor, the captive, the sick, and the brokenhearted.

When he was clearly and firmly established in his vocation in life, Jesus moved on to teach and heal in both synagogue and temple. His deeds and words were of a piece. He lived with complete integrity. And in so doing, he called and nurtured a small community of women and men to whom he gave great amounts of time and love (Luke 8:1-3), so that they, in turn, would learn how to be all that God meant them to be, how to use their gifts to show God's compassion to others, and how to teach God's truth with their words and lives.

In this stage of spiritual development, Jesus showed us by example the importance of putting our beliefs into practice on a daily basis, of integrating the will of God into our lives, of living a rhythm of solitude and prayer in the context of a small community of spiritual sharing, and of offering service to the larger community to which we are called.

Finally, Jesus established a relationship with God which meant that he sometimes had to challenge his own family, his own people, his own religious upbringing and its customs, and the authorities who ran the temple. He was not a "company man." Like his spiritual development, our spiritual development takes us (if we let it) beyond identification with the church and its institutional structures and traditions, in a movement toward increased faithfulness to the essence of God's will and a life of abiding in God and of God-like love for all — enemy and friend alike. This stage calls for a willingness to give and let go of our lives, to let them become like the grain of wheat falling into the ground.

Like Jesus, we are called to the cross — whatever form that may take. This cross is never something imposed on us by human custom or by other people or by accident. When we take it up in the way appropriate to this most mature stage of spiritual development, we always freely embrace it from a position of inner freedom and empowerment, just as Jesus freely embraced the cross.

It is clear that as Jesus went through the stages of human spiritual development, he did so far more fully and quickly than we do. He did not make the sinful choices we do. He had an unbroken and trusting relationship with God as "Abba," or "Papa," which we do not. Still, his development is a paradigm for ours, and the lives of many saints bear eloquent witness to this truth. Saint Francis, Saint Clare, Saint Benedict, Saint Teresa, and many others lived out the paradigm of development that Jesus modeled, each one in his or her own unique way, and often also reached a level of great spiritual maturity at a young age. This shows that there is no *necessary* correlation between age and stage of spiritual maturity, although there is certainly a common one!

Now that we have briefly reviewed the ancient wisdom of Scripture to give us a foundation for further discussion, it is time to examine a few of the developmental schemes that modern

120

students of human psychological and spiritual growth have described, in order to see how their descriptions also help us discern the way that is best for each of us to take nourishment at the Banqueting Table which God has prepared for us.

One of the pioneering descriptions of human development is that of Erik Erikson. Although his approach is psychological, many have seen the spiritual correlatives of his stages and have described them in books; one of them is *Pastoral Spirituality* by Ben Johnson.

The first stage is that of "trust versus mistrust." This crucial passage happens first in infancy. Our experience with parents and other caretakers influences whether or not we feel that we can trust others, or even life itself. If we are neglected or abused as infants and little children, it will be hard for us not only to trust others, but to trust ourselves, and to trust God. If we are wounded during this stage, that affects everything else in our spiritual development. Actually, all of us are on a kind of continuum where trust and mistrust are concerned. No one is likely to be totally trusting, since no one had perfect parents or caretakers. We all trust — more or less, depending on our particular circumstances. Therefore, we will "trust" ourselves to the prayers of the church, to the teachings of Scripture, to silence, to our senses and feelings, to our dreams and visions — more or less. To deal with this issue of trust, especially in relationship to God (which is not separate from our relationship to ourselves and others), is an ongoing and crucial task of spiritual growth. If we are not able to become more and more trusting, we will probably suffer from great spiritual emptiness.

The second stage is that of "autonomy versus dependence." This begins in childhood, but in our culture it continues through adolescence and early adulthood. If, as we grow older, we experience ourselves as being increasingly able to know and claim our own identity and power, we will have that wholesome sense of "self" or who we are that will enable us to relate to parents and others in a healthy, non–guilt-ridden way. In terms of spiritual development, this is the stage which is the necessary precondition to that later, mature stage when we are able to "deny ourselves." If we have never been allowed to pursue our own thoughts, ask our own questions, test our own abilities, and explore our own potential, we will have very little to later "deny."

Like all the other stages, this one is good and healthy if we don't get "stuck" in it for too long. If we do, we will alternate between compliance and rebellion with respect to authority figures and God. We will not be able to depend on our own inner resources and authority; we will always be looking outside ourselves for direction and affirmation. This produces an unhealthy spiritual and psychological dependence. Unfortunately, the structures and approach of some churches encourage this kind of dependence, with the clergy cast in the role of the parents — who are, of course, always necessary to the "children" or "sheep" in the congregation, who would be lost without their expert guidance!

The third stage, which is closely related to the second, is called "initiative versus passivity or conformity." (The names for these stages vary according to the sources consulted, but the dynamic is similar.) If one has developed a healthy autonomy of soul and spirit, one is able to take initiative and act out of one's own values, beliefs, and power, rather than being passively molded by those of others. This involves an increasing willingness to experiment and take risks, to test limits and possibilities, and, if necessary, to challenge the "powers that be" in one's life. From a spiritual standpoint, this passage needs to be negotiated in the context of a strong personal relationship with God and an ability to hear and follow the guidance of the Holy Spirit within the sanctuary of one's own heart. This passage offers the greatest possibility of integrity and stability, but it is also treacherous if one gets stuck here: acting out of one's own values and beliefs is a tricky thing if one is not clear about what these are and why, or if one has all sorts of conflicting and ambiguous notions about what one wants to do or be.

The fourth stage, which follows closely upon the third, is generativity: it has to do with developing a sense of one's own competence, gifts, and ability to contribute in a meaningful and satisfying way to the welfare of the human community in whatever ways best fit one's personality, circumstances, history, talents, and call. If one has not been able to take initiative and discover one's own values, beliefs, and abilities, it is hard to experience being a competent partner with others in ministry and work, or being a co-creator with God — or even a faithful servant. This stage and

122

the preceding two are often especially difficult for girls and women, since in this culture (and most others) they get ambiguous messages about being autonomous, taking initiative, challenging expectations about social roles, exercising their gifts, and the like. Nevertheless, it is fully as important for them as for boys and men to go through these stages if they are ever to be mature human beings and Christians. Both males and females suffer from a sense of inferiority and meaninglessness that is debilitating and depressing if they do not have a strong sense of their own unique gifts, competence, and contribution to society that goes beyond the social roles and stereotypes which so often serve as a prison of the soul and spirit.

The fifth stage, called "identity versus role confusion," calls for a deeply spiritual conviction that one is "God's beloved" and that one's identity is a gift of grace, symbolized (and some would say conveyed) by baptism. If someone has successfully gone through the preceding stages, this stage makes it possible for him or her to become free and mature enough to challenge society's traditional roles and to live in the freedom that Christ gives to each one who believes the truth about his or her real identity as image of God, child of God, friend of Christ, and sanctuary of the Holy Spirit. A person who succeeds in making this challenge develops a strong and unshakeable identity that goes far deeper than any role prescribed by society or expected by other people in his or her life.

It was this strong sense of identity, so clearly confirmed in his transfiguration experience, that enabled Christ to challenge the religious establishment and face the cross. So too, the deeper and stronger our sense of identity is, and the more rooted we are in who *God* says we are, the more we will be able to be true to our own unique nature and resist "being conformed to this world."

But we cannot do this alone. The sixth stage, called "intimacy versus isolation," involves marriage or some other form of intimate friendship, in the context of which we will live out our lives. The provision for intimacy in spiritual communities that has prevailed in the church through the centuries (even though many of the Protestant churches rejected the way it was often lived out in the Middle Ages) still provides an honorable alternative to marriage

123

for many Christians. The wisdom that needs to be discovered and lived out in this stage is that of maturing through covenanted relationships with others.

In relationships of genuine, honest love, mutuality, and intimacy, we are able to see both our gifts and our faults, and to experience the satisfaction of helping others grow as we grow. This is the stage of life in which we can be fruitful and generative, giving life to and supporting the flourishing of others (of whatever age) in an intentional and faithful way. We become mentors to others, and we are increasingly content to be "behind the scenes." If we are parents, we find that the task of parenting both expresses and equips us for this "generative" stage of life.

This leads, finally, to the last stage, integration, which often comes when we reach "senior citizen" status. This stage is the knitting together and culmination of all that has gone before. If one hasn't gotten stuck in an earlier stage, this stage is characterized by integrity, wisdom, patience, acceptance of self and others, and being at peace with one's life and sure of its meaning and worth. One has learned to forgive others — and most of all oneself — for faults and failures. One is able to face the future, even death, with hope rather than with despair. One is deeply aware of and grateful for the goodness of life. Those who are most likely to have reached this stage, of course, are those whose relationship with God has matured to the point of a deep faith and confidence in God's love and God's promise of eternal life. It also goes hand in hand with an acceptance of life's mystery and a sense of one's unity with God, with all people, and with creation. At the end of life it enables one to cry triumphantly with Christ, "It is finished!" and to whisper in trusting surrender, "Into your hands I commit my spirit."

Of course, this way of describing spiritual development is only one of many, and it is more age-related than some other schemas. It is also helpful to remember that the stages described above often overlap, and are not experienced in such neat and clear order as the description implies.

Another helpful schema that is not nearly so age-related is the one offered by Scott Peck in his book *The Different Drum*. Drawing on his extensive experience as a therapist and workshop leader, Peck describes adult spiritual growth in four basic stages.

The first stage is one characterized by self-centeredness, self-serving behavior, lack of integrity, manipulation of others, unprincipled and often hypocritical action — in short, "serving many gods," always for one's own benefit. Peck says such people often have a dark and chaotic inner life (described by Jesus as "full of corruption and decay, like a tomb"), even though the outside might look clean and neat — that is, "whitewashed." People in this stage have very little self-awareness, very little awareness of the true character, feelings, and needs of others, and very little genuine awareness of God. If they have an idea of divinity in their minds, it is usually a self-made idol, designed to further their own ends. They can do terrible things in the name of their "god" and think nothing of it. Nebuchadnezzar, as he is described in the book of Daniel, provides a good illustration of a person in this stage. Many Nazi leaders were in this first stage, as are other so-called modern leaders who claim to be religious while advocating violence and committing atrocities against others.

The second stage is characterized by a kind of conversion to some form of religious life in which the doctrinal, institutional, ritual, legal, and external aspects of religion are of utmost importance. Children raised in devout religious families often develop naturally into this stage. People in this stage frequently resist any changes in liturgy or custom. They accept what they are taught. They are often the majority of the "solid members" in any given congregation, and they place great value on dogma, on stability and continuity, and on the corporate rather than the interior, personal aspects of religion. In this stage they have a narrow, parochial outlook and are often judgmental of others who differ from them in belief, worship, or lifestyle. Generally, they are more interested in answers than in questions. They want and need the comfort of black-and-white rules and doctrines. Their concept of God is of One who is Lawgiver and Judge, who is transcendent, external, "high up," almighty, distant, and so on. They hold obedience and unquestioning faith in high regard. Not surprisingly, people in stage two are often the ones most willing to take on the tasks of running the religious institution and bearing the responsibilities of care-taking and maintenance. Many television preachers and their followers are in this stage of development, as well as people you probably know in the church you attend!

The third stage is characterized by skepticism, doubt, question-asking, and an ambiguous or downright anti-institutional stance toward religion. People going through this stage have faith, but it is a questing faith. They are no longer satisfied with the answers handed down to them. They are "truth seekers" who are usually passionate about social justice. These are the people who are often the church's severest critics — even if they stay connected to the church. Frequently, however, they go through a period when they leave the church completely and explore their own path for spiritual growth. Their concept of God is a constantly changing one, and they are often eclectic in their borrowing from the insights of different faiths. They are far more self-aware than people in stage one or stage two, and they are willing to take the risk and go through the pain of probing their own minds and hearts in their search for truth and in their passion for growth. Many members of the so-called baby-boom generation are in this stage; they have been dubbed "the New Believers" by sociologists of religion.

The fourth stage is characterized by a sense of the mystery of life. People in this stage have asked a lot of questions, searched hard for the answers, and discovered that there is a great deal beyond the reach of reason. They have gone deep into their hearts and found God there. They are self-aware and cognizant of the complexity and depth of their own nature. They have come to terms with their unique nature and their gifts, as well as their limits and faults. They are accepting of themselves, warts and all — and therefore are accepting of and open to others. They are not threatened by different views and lifestyles. They welcome dialogue with others about values and beliefs, and they are able and willing to lay aside their own preconceived notions and prejudices in order to be genuinely challenged, stretched, and even changed by others. They have a strong sense of the spiritual dimension of life and have discovered how to live contemplatively. They feel united with God and with others, and often with creation as well. Unlike stage-two people, who see God as distant, they see God primarily as the indwelling God, the Inner Light, the Holy Spirit, Christ within, and so on. They feel in constant communion with God, and because they have an increasing inner freedom, they feel increasingly free to let go of their external attachments to things and people and even to their own lives.

These overviews give you adequate outlines of Peck's much more detailed descriptions of these stages. But it is important to include one of the most important points Peck makes about these stages: that there is no automatic progression from one to the next. As he knows from his experience, a great many people never get beyond stage one. Many more stay in stage two their whole lives. Some go on to stage three. A minority — not very many — go on to stage four — and beyond, whatever that may be. Moreover, says Peck, those who do go on still have remnants of the previous stages in them, and they will often revert to those stages in crisis. To make matters even more complicated, most congregations have people in them in all four stages. People in stage two and stage four often seem most alike to the casual observer, but they are in church for almost opposite reasons.

People in the earlier stages are often threatened by people in the later stages, but people in the later stages can understand those in the earlier stages because they've been there. Much can be gained if people understand these stages, and give themselves and others permission to be wherever they are. It is helpful for everyone to remember that there is only One Judge, and that judging others is a burden we do not have to bear.

Nevertheless, Peck believes that the church must also try to help people progress from one stage to the next. This is difficult because people in stage two, who most often are running the church, are frequently threatened by people who need to go on to the critical third stage of doubting and challenging. Church leaders need to have faith in the maturation process, says Peck. If progress is not aborted by parents or church leaders and members, and if church members are surrounded by a loving community that is genuinely open and accepting, it is more likely that some of them will progress to stage four. It is such Christians who become the real "soul" and spiritual powerhouse of the church. Given the searching and struggling they have gone through, the depth of their prayer, love, and wisdom is of inestimable value to the church.

A less schematic way to describe adult spiritual growth is

simply to talk about the challenge of midlife. According to Carl Jung, this is the point at which we must explore the spiritual dimensions of life if we are to become generative and wise older people. At midlife, the challenge is to develop the unused or weaker aspects of our potential and personality. It is the time of life when we can, if we choose to, become more self-aware, experience God's promise: "My grace is sufficient for you, for my strength is made perfect in your weakness" (2 Cor. 12:9).

During the first half of life, we find and perfect our gifts. We make the most of our talents and strengths. We choose what is easiest and brings greatest reward — if we have a choice. During the first half of my life, for instance, I found that my greatest strengths lay in verbal communication, especially in public speaking. I developed this skill through college and used it often for years as I responded to numerous requests for speaking in various settings. Later, in seminary, I developed this gift more fully, along with gifts for research, writing, and theological reflection. I also discovered I had a strong gift for pastoral care, and I developed this as well. During my years as a pastor, I was able to use and further develop these gifts. This development of strengths and gifts in the first half of life is a fairly common pattern in the lives of many other people I know, and I see it clearly in the lives of my own adult children.

When midlife comes along, a great spiritual challenge comes with it. That challenge is to try to become whole, balanced, completed people who more fully develop the image of God within them by deliberately cultivating the less preferred ways of functioning that they have put aside, and the gifts that they may have neglected or repressed in order to carry out the choices of the first half of their lives. People who have reached this stage will often experience certain "symptoms" — troubling dreams, depression, dis-ease, and restlessness. These are signs of the need for a change, and a call to greater self-awareness and wholeness.

This is exactly what happened to me. As I neared the age of forty, I began to feel restless in my chosen vocation. I still enjoyed it and kept improving my skills as a pastor in various ways. But I began to have dreams that made me take a long, hard look at parts of me that needed to be developed — the part that loved solitude and silence and being behind the scenes rather than up front; and the part of me that was a frustrated artist. For years I had kept an easel, paints, brushes, and canvas paper in a storage area in my house. But somehow there was never enough time to "play" with these things. I also longed to write — not sermons, but poems and stories and books. But there was no time for that either in my busy life as pastor, mother, wife, and concerned citizen.

The restlessness, the urgent dreams, and the vague sense of dis-ease persisted. Finally, things reached a crisis stage, which often happens, especially when one isn't paying sufficient attention to the signals. When I went for a routine mammogram, it revealed the presence of breast cancer. The cancer was small and in its beginning stages. But it was a wake-up call. It became the catalyst for my realizing that I needed to develop the quiet, contemplative, prayerful, and artistic side of me before it was too late! In order to do that, I had to let go of a vocation and a way of using my strengths that was familiar, comfortable, rewarding, and with which I was deeply identified. It was the hardest thing I ever did. During the process I often felt like a trapeze artist in midswing: I had let go of one bar but hadn't yet grasped the other — I was simply flying through the air high above the ground with no safety net!

For me and for many others, choosing at midlife to take risks, try something new, and strike out in a new direction is all rather frightening. Sometimes it means giving up financial security and trusting God to provide the means necessary to follow the Spirit's leading. Yet, when we do, many can witness, as I have, that it is possible to follow one's heart and the deepest wisdom of one's being. In fact, if we are willing to make whatever changes are necessary — including changes in lifestyle — not only at midlife but through all the stages of life, no matter what age we are, we are set free in wonderful new ways to fulfill the purposes for which God created us.[1]

The important thing is to be able to discern what our age

1. For stories of people who have made such changes, see Marsha Sinetar's *Ordinary People as Monks and Mystics: Lifestyles for Self-Discovery* (Mahwah, N.J.: Paulist Press, 1986).

and stage in life call for in terms of our coming to the Banqueting Table of spiritual nourishment provided by God.

When it comes to receiving nourishment from worship at God's Feast, we might find that if we are in Scott Peck's stage two, we will need and want worship that is dependably the same and sermons that reassure us of our beliefs. If we are in Erikson's third stage of "initiative versus conformity," we might need to experiment by visiting different churches, starting a small worship group of our own, or taking courses that help us deal with all our questions in a satisfying way.

When we are children and teenagers, *lectio* can be just what we need if we concentrate on Bible stories that clearly connect with our lives and engage our lively imaginations. When we are in the last years of our lives, we may find ourselves needing a more contemplative kind of *lectio* that allows us to reflect on all we have learned in our lives, and the divine mystery we find in our lives and in Scripture.

Silence will probably be most appealing to us in the second rather than the first half of our lives, especially in this culture, in which children and youth are so constantly entertained and stimulated and given so little chance to experience silence. The fourth stage of development that Peck describes is one in which most people not only want but need silence like they need water and air. It is in silence that they most fully experience the presence of God, and their lives are most fruitful when they can be rooted in that silence in the very way they live from day to day.

Physical spirituality is something that people of all ages and stages can enjoy in a special sort of way. Children learn best through their senses, and when they are taught how to use their senses in a spiritual way, they really blossom. Teenagers often feel awkward and uncomfortable with their bodies and experience all sorts of confusion with respect to their sexuality. They can find a special benefit in a physical spirituality that encourages them to see their bodies as sacred and wonderful, and at the same time to see beauty and other desirable physical attributes as less important than spiritual beauty and strength.

The dreams and visions given by the Holy Spirit are probably most valuable to those who are in the later, most mature stages of spiritual growth and are therefore firmly rooted in their faith, open, and committed to discerning and following God's vision for their lives and the world. On the other hand, children love to pray with their imaginations — to enter into biblical stories, for instance, and pray with mental images. For example, children love to imagine that they are in the Ark with all those animals, or that they are giving Jesus their lunch to help him feed hungry people, like the boy did in the Gospel story about the feeding of the five thousand. Children also love to imagine that they are sitting in Jesus' lap, talking with him and listening to him and receiving his blessing. These activities can be very nourishing for them if they are guided and taught how to use their imaginations to commune with God and receive God's love.

The common thread that runs through all the ways of describing spiritual growth outlined in this chapter, and discerning how that growth affects the way to best enjoy God's Feast, is an increasing self-awareness, an increasing awareness of others, and an increasing awareness of God's loving presence and call in our lives. If we experience a growing inner freedom to respond to the love and call of God in all the ages and stages of our lives, we will be able to find just the nourishment we need at the Table so graciously provided by our loving Host. If we understand how we are personally affected by our age and stage in life as we sit at the Table, we will have the wisdom to eat wisely and well.

❋   ❋   ❋

Here are some specific spiritual exercises to help you further explore the material from this chapter and integrate it into your life:

1. Have you found any other helpful descriptions of the ages and stages of human development? Please describe them briefly. If not (or if you prefer to do this instead), reflect on your own observations of people's development. How would *you* describe the stages you have observed in yourself and others, especially from a spiritual perspective?
2. Using the biblical material in this chapter — particularly the

paradigm of Jesus' development — as a reference point, how would you describe your own *present* stage of spiritual development? How does your present age and stage affect your approach to each of the five "spiritual foods" described in the first five chapters of this book?

3. What insights about your own spiritual development did you gain from Erikson's seven stages as described in this chapter?

4. Try to find a Bible story or passage, a poem, a song (secular or sacred), or a prayer that illustrates each of the four stages that Peck describes. Or write your own illustration of each. Or use art to express each one. Your choice!

Books for Further Reference

1. *Christian Life Patterns: The Psychological Challenges and Religious Invitations of Adult Life* and *Seasons of Strength: New Visions of Adult Christian Maturing* by Evelyn E. Whitehead and James D. Whitehead
Each of these books is a thorough and enlightening study of the spiritual and psychological stages of adult maturation. In each the Whiteheads offer many illuminating examples and much wisdom for negotiating the passages they describe.

2. *Celebrate Mid-Life* by Janice Brewi and *Mid-Life Directions: Praying and Playing Sources of New Dynamism* by Janice Brewi and Anne Brennan
These two books take a close look at what happens to women and men in our culture when they reach midlife (both the similarities and the differences), and the dangers and possibilities of this important phase of human development. There are many questions that invite personal reflection as well as examples that illustrate how to celebrate midlife.

3. *The Spiritual Life of Children* by Robert Coles
This much-acclaimed book is a wonderful exploration of how children live a spiritual life, and their fresh and unique perspectives on religious and spiritual matters. It is based on extensive,

132

sensitively conducted interviews with children; much of the material is rendered in their own words.

4. *The Different Drum: Community-Making and Peace* by M. Scott Peck
In this book Peck thoroughly describes the four stages of human development that I have specifically referred to in this chapter. His extensive observations undergird his thoughtful conclusions about how we need to live in community together.

5. *The Hunger of the Heart: A Call to Spiritual Growth* by Ron DelBene with Herb Montgomery
In this small, simple, but profound book, DelBene, who is a pastor, teacher, and spiritual director to many, describes the stages of the spiritual journey that he has observed in his directees and in himself over the years. His descriptions are clear and helpful for all those who wonder if they are making any progress, or are alone in what they are experiencing.

CHAPTER 9

Grounded in Gender

Vive la différence!" say the French about the differences between men and women. "Why can't a woman be more like a man?" asks Professor Higgins in the musical *My Fair Lady.* "Oh God, I thank Thee that Thou didst not make me a woman," says an old rabbinical prayer. Such sentiments about the differences between the sexes have persisted for centuries. But only recently have these differences been examined and articulated by a number of women with psychological, sociological, and theological training in a way that has received widespread attention.

Previously, the differences between male and female when it came to spirituality were scarcely noticed. The differences that were described were most often what men observed and then ascribed to "the nature of women." At the same time, when it came to things religious and spiritual, human nature and understanding were equated with male nature and understanding.

Today, as women and men have become increasingly aware of their own spirituality in a way that is connected to and expressive of all aspects of their being and experience, the authentic differences between male and female are becoming clearer. The fact that the nature of our relationship to God, and therefore our spirituality, is grounded in gender is now beyond dispute. The implications of this truth are still being explored.

It has become apparent that one of the root problems which has resulted in the lack of understanding of the differences between male and female spirituality is that of the dualisms between body and spirit, male and female, humanity and creation. This dualism is in itself a sinful way of thinking, and it has had sad consequences. In order to live and die happily, says the Heidelberg Catechism (one of the most important documents of the Reformation), we must first know how great our sins and misery (or alienation) are.

The story of the Fall clearly shows the process by which human beings fell from a state of loving and trusting communion with God, each other, and creation, into a state of suspicion and alienation. Once Adam and Eve believed the lie that God did not really have their good at heart and then acted accordingly, their bodies became a source of shame and pain. Their relationship deteriorated into one of domination and submission, and the earth became a burden of toil and frustration. Adam and Eve became alienated from God, each other, their bodies, and creation.

One result of the alienation between body and spirit is an understanding of spirituality that is often dis-embodied. Until recently, very little has been written in the West about the profound way in which our bodies affect our souls, our spirits, and the way we relate to God, others, and ourselves. Most of the writers in the Western Christian tradition have taken a decidedly negative view of the body, often perceiving it and the sexuality of human beings as enemies of the spiritual life. In this way they have departed from the Jewish roots of Christianity and reflected the influence of Greek philosophy. The ideal became conquering the body's urges and more or less beating it into submission with ascetic practices.

Along with this approach there developed a misogynist attitude toward women, who were regarded as more earthy, sexual, bodily creatures than men. Women were regarded and portrayed as temptresses, and their bodily functions were often considered "unclean." Some church fathers even wondered out loud if women had souls; almost all agreed that they were less "images of God" than men were. Naturally, women's spirituality did not exactly flourish in this sort of atmosphere!

Fortunately, there has been a good deal of change in the church, and in the second half of this century, there is a far healthier attitude toward the body and sexuality. And the view of women as inferior is slowly fading away. Nevertheless, there is still a great deal that needs to be done in terms of honoring women's experience and spirituality equally with that of men — on the part of both men and women.

As women find their voice and express their own authentic spirituality, men are also exploring what is unique to male spirituality. Both women and men are drawing profound connections between their bodies, their lived experience, and the way they relate to themselves, others, God, and creation.

The differences between men and women that are being uncovered and articulated are both biological-genetic and cultural-environmental. Naturally, there is still a great deal of debate about which differences are "innate" and which are "conditioned." The relationship between the two is so complex that we will probably never know which is which in any conclusive way. For, after all, we are looking at ourselves, and the reflection we see is strongly influenced by many unconscious factors. The most accurate assessment emerges when the reflections made by women and men from many different cultures and ways of life are put together. Then the commonalities become more clear, along with the biases and the differences.

Men and women do have many similarities, for we are human together. But there are important differences too — in hormonal systems, body build, sexual organs, even in brain structure. All of these affect our spirituality. Women's close relationship to the waxing and waning of the moon through the menstrual cycle makes many of them feel connected to creation in an elemental way. As they claim their right to honor this in their spirituality, it will give their spirituality a shape different from that of male spirituality. In addition, the fact that women can — and often do — carry babies inside their bodies, give birth, and nurse babies gives them a particular set of physical experiences that are the basis for corresponding spiritual experiences.

Men also have unique influences, including their physical experiences as hunters, warriors, protectors, and providers in many cultures, and their bodily experience of the involuntary arousal of their sexual organ and its external position on their bodies. Perhaps the greater aggressiveness and need for control that seem to characterize much of male behavior are related to these experiences

137

and influences. The fact that spiritual literature written by men is filled with images of control, penetration, and up-down hierarchical concepts supports this view.

The cultural differences between men and women are harder to universalize, but they certainly can be described in terms of (for instance) Western American culture. There are clear expectations and models for male and female "nature" and behavior that profoundly shape men and women. Men are supposed to be natural leaders; they are also supposed to be stronger, tougher, less emotional, and more intellectual than women. In our culture, they bond more by doing things together than by just being together and talking, as women do. Women are supposed to be natural followers; they are also supposed to be weaker, more emotional, and less intellectual than men. In addition, they are supposed to look "feminine" and act "feminine" — that is, be attractive to men. There is a "masculine" way to look and dress too, but it has less to do with attracting women than with "being male." In art and the media, men are more often portrayed as the major actors in society. Conversely, women are more often portrayed as objects to be looked at and used, or the less important partners or "love interests" in men's lives.

These and many other stereotypes infiltrate the faith and life of Christians in a way that profoundly influences the spirituality of women and men. For this reason, men and women will approach the Feast that God has prepared for them in quite different ways.

For example, men's concept of God generally emphasizes God's transcendence — God is "out there" or "up there." God is imaged as male — Father and Son. The Holy Spirit is also considered male (though the name does not imply maleness as "Father" and "Son" do). Terms like "king," "ruler," and "Lord" are important, along with the concepts of submission, obedience, and obeisance, which indicate the ideal way of relating to God. Many of the prayers of the church reveal these concepts.

From women's point of view, these concepts exhibit a certain formality and distance. Most women tend to relate more to the immanence of God — God with us, God the Holy Spirit within us. Since women have wombs, and many have the experience of carrying another person inside them, it makes sense that they relate more easily to this aspect of God. The artist and author Meinrad Craighead expresses what many women experience in this way:

> God the Mother came to me when I was a child and, as children will do, I kept her a secret. We hid together inside the structures of institutional Catholicism. . . . This natural religious instinct for my Mothergod gave me a profound sense of security and stability. She was the sure ground I grew in, the groundsill of my spirituality. Yet we remained comfortably at home in the bosom of Holy Mother Church. My Catholic heritage and environment have been like a beautiful river flowing over my subterranean foundation in God the Mother. The two movements are not in conflict, they simply water different layers in my soul. This personal vision of God the Mother, incarnated in my mother and her mother, gave me, from childhood, the clearest certainty of women as the truer image of Divine Spirit. Because she was a force living within me, she was more real, more powerful than the remote Fathergod I was educated to have faith in. I believed in her because I experienced her. Instinctively I knew that this private vision needed protecting; my identity, my very life depended on its integrity.[1]

Many more women today are finding their spiritual nurture — and self-esteem — restored when they realize that they image God as fully as men do, and that therefore God is as appropriately imaged and named in feminine ways as in masculine ways. Those women (and they are legion) who have been sexually, physically, emotionally, and spiritually abused as children and adults by men often find it difficult to relate to God as male, at least until they have consciously worked through the pain of their abuse and experienced significant healing.

Other women, though they may not have been personally abused in such awful ways, are increasingly uncomfortable relating to the solely male God depicted by the patriarchal cultural influence in Christianity. Other images of God feed their souls: Spirit,

---

1. Craighead, introduction to *The Mother's Songs: Images of God the Mother* (Mahwah, N.J.: Paulist Press, 1985).

Comforter, Friend, loving Mother. As women increasingly recognize their distinctive awareness of God, and as that awareness is articulated and then accepted in the church, a better balance is developing between the ways men and women image God and relate to God. As both men and women become able to see the feminine as well as the masculine face of God, the image of God is gradually losing its idolatrous identification with maleness. Of course, thoughtful men and women realize that God is far beyond what any images can convey, including images of maleness and femaleness.

Gender affects not only the different ways men and women are aware of and relate to God, but also the way they feast at the Banquet to which God invites them. For there is food on the Table that has been "cooked up" mainly by men, who have authored the Scriptures, shaped and led the church's worship, and created most of its "official" history, theology, and tradition. It is not surprising, then, that women and men often find themselves choosing and receiving God's spiritual nourishment in different ways.

The church's liturgy, for instance, feels far more comfortable to most men than to many women. The imagery in hymns, prayers, and the kinds of rituals and theology that are part of worship have a strong masculine cast. Increasingly, women are feeling uncomfortable with the lack of feminine imagery, language, theology, and ritual. As women finally claim their right to name religious experience and to worship in ways that fit them, they are re-creating the worship and prayer of the church so that it can be nourishing for them.

More and more men are enjoying the feminine dimension of liturgy as well, and finding that it also nourishes *their* souls. Clearly, the more the church and each congregation become able to provide the kind of liturgy that nourishes both masculine and feminine sensitivities and needs, the better the Feast will be.

As women these days try *lectio* using Scripture, they find that many parts of the Bible have been culturally conditioned by a patriarchal outlook and masculine perspective. In the Old Testament, for example, women are treated unequally under the law and are clearly regarded as possessions. One of the Ten Commandments says, "Thou shalt not covet thy neighbor's wife, or his ox,

140

or his ass." Most interpretations of the Fall in Genesis have laid the blame at women's door, and have decreed the domination that was the result of the Fall as the inevitable and proper fate of womankind as a punishment for Eve's sin. Although these things are not said anymore in many Christian circles, their echoes linger in the air.

When women ingest these interpretations along with the passages, they get a bad stomachache! They also ache when they notice how few women's perspectives and accomplishments are recorded in salvation history, and how few feminine images of God survive in the text, compared with the abundance of masculine perspectives, accomplishments, images, and language.

To make matters worse, women have experienced being stifled and confined by certain verses from the epistles which, though few in number, have been used as a weapon against them to keep them in "their place." It is no wonder, then, that women have a harder time eating the "bread" of Scripture than men do, although sensitive men today are having the same problem.

Fortunately, women can always turn to the good nourishment of the Gospels. In Jesus' words and deeds there is no trace of the common patriarchal tendency to overlook, denigrate, or patronize women. On the contrary, Jesus deliberately defied conventions that oppressed women in order to minister to them. He welcomed them as his disciples. He was intimate with them without using them sexually. He found them to be his truest friends, for they did not betray or forsake him as did the male disciples. And he made them the first witnesses of the Resurrection and the first apostles of the power of the risen Christ.

But women can and are turning to parts of the Bible beyond the Gospels as well, for they are discovering, through careful study and reflection, the important role of women in the Bible, and are bringing hitherto hidden feminine perspectives to light. In our generation, women scholars, teachers, writers, and preachers are transforming the male-oriented interpretive tradition of the past so that Scripture can speak God's Word of love, justice, and freedom to them as well.

When it comes to physical spirituality, women usually have less difficulty than they do with traditional liturgy and scriptural

141

interpretation. Their biological experiences as women help them live in tune with their bodies and their senses. For many women, the experiences of childbearing, birthing, and nursing are profound sensuous-spiritual experiences of communion and cooperation with God in the sacred task of bringing forth and nurturing new life. Even those women who do not physically bear children are often powerfully in sync with nature and find that they commune with God most deeply through creation and their senses.

Men also have this experience; but it is certainly true that because men and women have different bodies, and because they sense things differently and value sensory experience differently, men's physical spirituality is different from women's. As both men and women discover and explore these differences, they will be able to enjoy physical spirituality in their own unique ways with greater wisdom and appreciation.

Silence is equally fruitful in the lives of men and women. Both of them need times of solitude to commune with God and honor the needs of their souls. The differences come in how they seek this solitude — and it must be actively sought, because American culture does not honor this need in the lives of men or women.

Men often need to have an excuse — like going hunting or fishing — which allows them to be alone and in silence if they so choose. Even then, they most often go hunting or fishing with a group, even if they end up spending a few hours alone in the woods or on a river. This "grouping" tendency is culturally conditioned and protects men from the stigma of saying they want to be alone. If any man, except perhaps a priest or a pastor, expressed a desire to spend time alone in silence in order to pray, he would probably meet with a great deal of misunderstanding and even downright scorn.

Women, on the other hand, often find that no excuse is good enough to give them adequate time for silence. The multiple demands of their lives — as daughters, sisters, wives, mothers, church volunteers, community volunteers, friends, and workers — seem to crowd out personal time. What compounds the problem is that their upbringing usually makes them feel selfish if they do take time just for themselves, because part of the cultural expectation for women is that they are always available — to men, to children, to anyone in need. Going to the beauty shop and the shopping mall seem to be the only acceptable "self-indulgent" activities.

Without a doubt, both women and men need to make persistent efforts in different ways to claim "sabbath time" for themselves. Perhaps because of cultural conditioning, women more easily go "inward" when they do have an opportunity to spend some time in silence; more men seem to resist this or have trouble with it. But the fact that men in certain other cultures find it very attractive and very possible to enter deeply into silence and solitude seems to indicate that American culture is the major culprit that prevents men from enjoying the spiritual nurture of silence. Enjoying silence, which can seem like a passive activity, is difficult in a culture that teaches men to be "doers."

Unfortunately, as more and more women enter the male-shaped systems of the working-for-wages world, this cultural ideal is increasingly keeping women from enjoying the fruits of silence as well. So both women and men need to resist the cultural messages that confine them, and help each other claim the time and find safe and nourishing spaces for the experience of solitude and silence in communion with God.

Visions and dreams, also principal foods of God's Feast, are nourishing for women as well as men. At Pentecost, the Holy Spirit gave the gift of dreams and visions to women and men alike. When they are attentive to their own visions and dreams, they experience a profound communion with and guidance by the presence of the Holy Spirit within them. This guidance often puts them at odds not only with the culture but also with some of the traditions of the church. Women may feel led into ministry in denominations or congregations that do not welcome women in pastoral leadership. Men may feel led into vocations such as nursing or child care, even though this defies cultural stereotypes about men. These days, both men and women are being called through dreams and visions to live in a way that challenges their families, their churches, their traditions, and their communities to change, so that both sexes might fully use their gifts and freedom as people who image God and do not need to live by social stereotypes.

As women articulate their dreams and visions in art and in

music and in words, certain fascinating patterns are emerging. These patterns are revealing the special characteristics of women's images, imaginations, and souls. The uniqueness of women's dreams and visions is important to notice, because the dreams and visions coming from the souls of men — revealed in art, in myth-making, poetry, and other literature, in music, in architecture, and so on — have dominated and shaped most cultures for millennia. Here too, the assumption has been that "male" equals "human."

As a result, both men and women have been cheated, because they have not been able to realize or appreciate the differences between them in the realm of psyche and spirit. Therefore, they have not been able to learn from what is unique and different in the other gender's visions and dreams. As both American culture and the church are increasingly influenced by the articulated visions and dreams of women, there will be a far greater richness of beauty, wisdom, and truth available to everyone.

In light of the differences between men and women noted above and how they affect the way men and women feast at the Banqueting Table, it seems appropriate to note that the differences between men and women (as well as the other factors explored in the earlier chapters in this section) need to be carefully observed and honored in spiritual direction. When men give spiritual counsel and guidance to women, they need to avoid pressing women into a male mold. In order to give genuinely nurturing guidance, they need to be keenly aware of the differences between women and men and how they affect female and male spirituality. They need to encourage women to reflect upon their own experience, intuition, and "gut sense" of what seems right. They must help women claim their freedom in Christ to break free from cultural stereotypes, and they must challenge the tendency of many women to comply, please, and submit in ways that do violence to themselves.

Of course, the reverse is also true. Women who give spiritual direction to men also need to encourage men to break free of cultural stereotypes of masculinity, many of which contradict the values and example of Jesus as taught in the Gospels. They need to challenge the tendency of many men to dominate, to ignore their own feelings as well as those of others, and to live by a double standard, especially in the sexual realm. In short, wise spiritual directors will always take into account the fact that women and men struggle with different issues in different ways in their spiritual development.

On the other hand, it is also true that "In Christ there is neither . . . male nor female . . . for all are one in Christ Jesus" (Gal. 3:28). There are many commonalities that men and women share in their spirituality, as well as in other aspects of their being and life. Both are made in the image of God, and both have been equally redeemed and set free by Christ from the guilt and power of sin of every kind. Both are indwelt and empowered by the Holy Spirit to become all they were meant to be, whole and holy, like Christ in love and goodness. Both are called to mature into their full humanity, which means that men need to develop certain qualities typically called "feminine," and women need to develop certain qualities typically called "masculine." The spiritual food that God provides at the Banqueting Table is intended to help women and men alike grow in grace and knowledge, and walk with God in a way that is redemptive for their families, their churches and communities, and the whole world.

❋   ❋   ❋

Here are a few exercises to help you to integrate the material in this chapter into your life:

1. Reflect on (and write about) how the fact that you are a woman or a man influences the way *you* find your spiritual nourishment. Try reflecting on a different "food" from the Feast each day. To gain more insight into how differences in gender affect our spirituality, you may find it helpful to consult *Women at the Well: Feminist Perspectives on Spiritual Direction* by Kathleen Fischer and *The Intimate Connection: Male Sexuality, Masculine Spirituality* by James B. Nelson.
2. Imagine and describe in your journal what the church would be like if women and men were equally honored, their gifts and perspectives equally accepted, and their differences equally respected and cherished.

145

3. Try these experiments: (a) Image God as female, then male. Write a prayer to God in each case, and notice the differences between them. (b) Read a Scripture passage and substitute female pronouns for the masculine pronouns used for God and males; see how you react. (c) Reflect on some typical masculine images from Scripture and the Christian tradition — for example, Jacob's ladder, the Bible as a sword, God as a warrior, fortress, or shield, and so on. What would be some equivalent feminine images that would convey similar meaning?

4. Look through a hymnbook and notice the prevalence of male language and images in many hymns. Try rewriting one with female language and images. Reflect on your response. (In *What Language Shall I Borrow?* Brian Wren takes a helpful look at the masculinization of church hymnody and its consequences, and suggests concrete ways to remedy the situation.)

Books for Further Reference

1. *Women's Reality: An Emerging Female System in the White Male Society* by Anne Wilson Schaef
This pioneering book by a well-known woman therapist and writer explores how women of all kinds see reality in ways that are quite different from the ways in which reality is depicted by the culture's "white male system." The book is filled with eye-opening examples of how different the two realities are, and what a significant difference this makes for people.

2. *Women at the Well: Feminist Perspectives on Spiritual Direction* by Kathleen Fischer
The whole matter of women's spirituality is beautifully explored in this irenic and healing book. It will help both women and men understand women's spirituality and its relationship to everyday life. The exercises and questions after each chapter are

developed in such a way that the book can be used by an individual or a group.

3. *The Intimate Connection: Male Sexuality, Masculine Spirituality* by James B. Nelson
In this book, Nelson explores masculine spirituality in our culture in a most enlightening and stimulating way. For all those interested in knowing more about the differences between women and men, this book makes a good complement to the two books listed above.

4. *What Language Shall I Borrow? God-Talk in Worship: A Male Response to Feminist Theology* by Brian Wren
The author, a minister of the Reformed Church and a well-known hymnwriter, explores the assumptions of church hymnody and its reflection of patriarchal attitudes in its strongly masculine imagery and language. Wren reviews history, and with great reason and patience he shows how things got to be the way they are, why change is needed, and how it can come about so that church music is equally hospitable to women and men.

5. *In Her Own Rite: Constructing Feminist Liturgical Tradition* by Marjorie Procter-Smith
This fine little book examines the work that women theologians and liturgists are doing, and need to do, as they work to transform the traditional worship of the church into worship that fits women and men well and is genuinely pastoral and inclusive. Procter-Smith offers thoughtful insights and practical suggestions for those who are interested in such reform.

6. *WomanPrayer, WomanSong: Resources for Ritual, Liturgies, Songs; WomanWisdom: A Feminist Lectionary and Psalter on Women of the Hebrew Scriptures, Part I; WomanWitness: A Feminist Lectionary and Psalter on Women of the Hebrew Scriptures, Part II; and WomanWord: A Feminist Lectionary and Psalter on Women of the New Testament* by Miriam Therese Winters
This well-known Medical Mission Sister, a Catholic with great

musical talent and liturgical skill, has written these groundbreaking volumes in order to show what prayer and worship are like
when done in a truly womanly fashion that reflects women's
spirituality in a Christian context. These books are wonderful
resources for women and men who want to explore these new
ways of worship.

7. *Swallow's Nest: A Feminine Reading of the Psalms* by Marchiene Vroon Rienstra
   This book uses feminine language to paraphrase the Psalms in
   a way that allows them to be used for daily prayer by individuals
   or groups. It also includes an appendix of readings by women
   church leaders. *Swallow's Nest* is designed to help people explore
   worship that honors the feminine.

Conclusion

"It is not so much that the Jews have kept the Sabbath as that the Sabbath has kept the Jews" says a well-known rabbinical quotation. It points to what has kept the heart and soul and identity of the Jewish people alive: the setting aside of a significant block of time (a full day — twenty-four hours — every seven days) to cease from everyday labors and concerns and instead to worship God, ponder God's Word, rest in God's presence, and commune with God.

It would probably not be too much to say that keeping Sabbath — regularly taking a significant period of time to feast at the Table of spiritual nourishment that God provides — is also essential for our spiritual survival as Christians in a society which constantly distracts and pressures us so that we forget who we really are and what we are here for. This is true for us as individuals who bear God's image and who might gain the whole world but lose our own souls if we do not keep Sabbath. And it is true for us as God's people — a "royal priesthood, a holy nation" that has been called and formed for God's glory and saving purposes for the whole creation. Keeping the Sabbath of regular worship and communion with God is the way we keep ourselves open to being transformed by God's Word and Spirit rather than conformed to the mold of the status quo. It is giving one of the most precious gifts we have, which is time, to the One who has given us everything we have.

It is so obvious! Without "Sabbath" time, we cannot "come to the Banquet." We rob ourselves of the Feast that God prepares for us. We become malnourished and empty inside because the "fast food" we grab on the run is neither nourishing nor fulfilling. The parable of the great banquet that Jesus tells in Luke 14:15-24 is both an invitation and a warning. It is a warm, inviting, and open invitation to all from the heart of God our Host: "Come, for everything is ready now" (Luke 14:17). But for those who say they are too busy to come, there is a warning: If they will not make time and room in their lives to come to the Feast and sit at the Banqueting Table with God and God's other invited guests, they will find that someday they will not be able to feast at all.

It is my fervent hope and prayer that each of you who reads this book will come to the Feast over and over again, and there find the nourishment for your soul that will strengthen you to go out from the banqueting hall ready and fit for the work and witness to which God calls you. For there is a holy rhythm of coming to the Feast and going out into the world again that needs to be honored. For some, the temptation might be to spend too much time and eat too much at the Table. For many others, the temptation is to keep on going even after their spiritual strength is gone and their souls' reserves are depleted. Then they wonder why God seems far away, faith seems irrelevant, and they have so little energy and joy in their hearts!

It may be that the command to keep Sabbath is a sensible rhythm and guide for many of us: six days of labor, service, and involvement in the world; and one full day — from sunset to sunset, or sunrise to sunrise — during which we feast at the Banqueting Table, sampling the varieties of "soul food" described in this book, either in solitude or with others. This might demand that we sacrifice watching television, going shopping, or pursuing other activities that prevent us from spending a truly nourishing amount of time at the Table.

However, the rewards of coming to the Table are far greater than those of any activity we might substitute for that experience. There is a joy, an energy, a spiritual vitality, a wellspring of creativity, refreshment, and comfort that restores our souls during true "Sabbath time." We experience a foretaste of the blessing of communion with God which, by the testimony of multitudes of believers through the ages, is greater than anything else in life. God's invitation to you stands. Will you come to the Feast? When will you set aside "Sabbath time"? Daily? Weekly? Monthly or yearly?

And will you let others know of the Feast that awaits them too? Will you encourage them to come with you? For our generous and gracious Host says, "Go out and urge people to come in, so that my House may be filled" (Luke 14:23). People all around us are hungry, not so much for institutional religion as for a personal experience of God — the kind of intimate knowing that the Bible defines as being like the loving intimacy between a husband and wife. Even more important than telling people *about* God (which is often called "evangelism") is inviting them to come with you to the Feast to which God invites all who are hungry and thirsty for something more.

The earliest Christians first experienced God by knowing Jesus Christ and by receiving the Holy Spirit. In the ways described in this book (and more), they came to know God in a vital, personal way that transformed their lives. Reflection, and the doctrine born of it, came after the experience.

I believe it is vitally important that churches become Banqueting Tables to which all are sincerely invited and warmly welcomed, and where all are amply fed with the experiential spiritual nourishment that God provides. And I believe it is vitally important that each of us eats at the Table with an invited guest. Then God's House will be full as never before, and it will be a place of joyful celebration, because we, as individuals and churches, have put first things first!

Resources for Further Study and Experience

Recommended Books

Allchin, A. M., ed. *Solitude and Communion: Papers on the Hermit Life*. Convent of the Incarnation, Fairacres, Oxford: S. L. G. Press.

Beagle, J. Robert. *A Guide to Monastic Guest Houses*. Wilton, Conn.: Morehouse Publishing, 1989.

Bellah, Robert N., et al. *Habits of the Heart: Individualism and Commitment in American Life*. New York: Harper & Row, 1986.

The Book of Common Prayer. New York: Seabury Press, 1979.

Brewi, Janice. *Celebrate Mid-Life*. New York: Crossroad, 1989.

————, and Anne Brennan. *Mid-Life Directions: Praying and Playing Sources of New Dynamism*. Mahwah, N.J.: Paulist Press, 1985.

Brother Lawrence and Frank Laubach. *Practicing His Presence*. Beaumont, Tex.: The Seed Sources, 1973.

Bynum, Caroline W., et al. *Gender and Religion: On the Complexity of Symbols*. Boston: Beacon Press, 1986.

Byzantine Book of Prayer. Pittsburgh: Byzantine Seminary Press, 1976.

152

Coles, Robert. *The Spiritual Life of Children*. Boston: Houghton Mifflin, 1990.

DelBene, Ron, et al. *The Breath of Life: A Simple Way to Pray*. Nashville: Upper Room, 1992.

————, with Herb Montgomery. *The Hunger of the Heart: A Call to Spiritual Growth*. Nashville: Upper Room, 1992.

de Mello, Anthony. *Sadhana: A Way to God: Christian Exercises in Eastern Form*. Saint Louis: Institute of Jesuit Sources, 1978.

————. *Wellsprings: A Book of Spiritual Exercises*. New York: Doubleday, 1985.

Doberstein, John W., ed. *Minister's Prayer Book: An Order of Prayers and Readings*. Philadelphia: Fortress Press, 1986.

Doherty, Catherine. *Poustinia*. Notre Dame: Ave Maria Press, 1975.

Fischer, Kathleen. *Women at the Well: Feminist Perspectives on Spiritual Direction*. Mahwah, N.J.: Paulist Press, 1988.

Foreman, Ellen. *Awakening: A Dream Journal*. 2 vols. New York: Stewart, Tabori & Chang, 1988.

Fox, Matthew. *On Becoming a Musical, Mystical Bear: Spirituality American Style*. Paramus, N.J.: Paulist Press, 1976.

Franck, Frederick. *The Zen of Seeing*. New York: Random House, 1973.

Gilligan, Carol. *In a Different Voice: Psychological Theory and Women's Development*. Cambridge: Harvard University Press, 1982.

Grant, Harold, et al. *From Image to Likeness: A Jungian Path in the Gospel Journey*. Ramsey, N.J.: Paulist Press, 1983.

Harris, Maria. *Dance of the Spirit: The Seven Steps of Women's Spirituality*. New York: Doubleday–Bantam Books, 1989.

Hays, Edward. *Pray All Ways*. Easton, Kans.: Forest Peace, 1981.

————. *Secular Sanctity*. Rev. ed. Easton, Kans.: Forest Peace, 1984.

Johnson, Ben C. *Pastoral Spirituality: A Focus for Ministry*. Philadelphia: Westminster Press, 1988.

Johnson, Robert A. *Inner Work: Using Dreams and Active Imagination for Personal Growth*. New York: Harper & Row, 1986.

Keating, Thomas. *The Mystery of Christ: The Liturgy as Spiritual Experience.* Rockport, Mass.: Element, Inc., 1991.

———. *Open Mind, Open Heart: The Contemplative Dimension of the Gospel.* Rockport, Mass.: Element, Inc., 1991.

Kelsey, Morton T. *The Other Side of Silence: A Guide to Christian Meditation.* Paramus, N.J.: Paulist Press, 1976.

Kiersey, David, and Marilyn Bates. *Please Understand Me: Character and Temperament Types.* Buffalo, N.Y.: Prometheus Books, 1978.

Linn, Dennis, and Matthew Linn. *Healing Life's Hurts: Healing Memories through the Five Stages of Forgiveness.* New York: Paulist Press, 1978.

Merton, Thomas. *New Seeds of Contemplation.* New York: New Directions, 1961.

Michael, Chester P., and Marie C. Norrisey. *Prayer and Temperament: Different Prayer Forms for Different Personality Types.* Charlottesville, Va.: Open Door, Inc., 1984.

Miller, Alice. *Thou Shalt Not Be Aware: Society's Betrayal of the Child.* New York: NAL/Dutton, 1986.

Nelson, James B. *The Intimate Connection: Male Sexuality, Masculine Spirituality.* Philadelphia: Westminster Press, 1988.

Nouwen, Henri J. *Behold the Beauty of the Lord: Praying with Icons.* Notre Dame: Ave Maria Press, 1987.

———. *Out of Solitude.* Notre Dame: Ave Maria Press, 1974.

O'Connor, Elizabeth. *Eighth Day of Creation: Discovering Your Gifts and Using Them.* Waco, Tex.: Word Books, 1971.

———. *Search for Silence.* Waco, Tex.: Word Books, 1972.

Pais, Janet. *Suffer the Children.* Mahwah, N.J.: Paulist Press, 1991.

Peck, M. Scott. *The Different Drum: Community-Making and Peace.* New York: Simon & Schuster, 1987.

Pennington, M. Basil. *Centering Prayer: Renewing an Ancient Christian Prayer Form.* Garden City, N.Y.: Doubleday, 1982.

People's Prayer Book. New York: Catholic Book Publishing Co., 1980.

Pobee, John S., and Barbel Von Wartenberg-Potter, eds. *New Eyes for Reading: Biblical and Theological Reflections by Women from the Third World.* New York: Meyer-Stone Books, 1987.

Postema, Donald H. *Space for God: The Study and Practice of*

Spirituality and Prayer. Grand Rapids: CRC Publications, 1983.

Procter-Smith, Marjorie. *In Her Own Rite: Constructing Feminist Liturgical Tradition.* Nashville: Abingdon Press, 1990.

Rienstra, Marchiene Vroon. *Swallow's Nest: A Feminine Reading of the Psalms.* Grand Rapids: William B. Eerdmans, 1992.

Russell, Letty M., ed. *Changing Contexts of Our Faith.* Philadelphia: Fortress Press, 1985.

Sager, Allan H. *Gospel-Centered Spirituality: An Introduction to Our Spiritual Journey.* Minneapolis: Augsburg Fortress, 1990.

Sanford, Agnes. *The Healing Light.* New York: Ballantine Books, 1983.

———, ed. *The Healing Gifts of the Spirit.* New York: Harper & Row, 1984.

Sanford, John A. *Dreams: God's Forgotten Language.* New York: Harper & Row, 1989.

———. *The Kingdom Within: The Inner Meaning of Jesus' Sayings.* Rev. ed. San Francisco: Harper & Row, 1987.

Savary, Louis M., and Patricia H. Berne. *Kything: The Art of Spiritual Presence.* Mahwah, N.J.: Paulist Press, 1988.

Savary, Louis M., Strephon Kaplan Williams, and Patricia H. Berne. *Dreams and Spiritual Growth: A Christian Approach to Dreamwork.* Mahwah, N.J.: Paulist Press, 1984.

Schaef, Anne Wilson. *Women's Reality: An Emerging Female System in the White Male Society.* New York: Harper & Row, 1985.

Schmemann, Alexander. *For the Life of the World: Sacraments and Orthodoxy.* Crestwood, N.Y.: St. Vladimir's Seminary Press, 1973.

Sinetar, Marsha. *Ordinary People as Monks and Mystics: Lifestyles for Self-Discovery.* Mahwah, N.J.: Paulist Press, 1986.

Underhill, Evelyn. *Worship.* New York: Crossroad, 1982.

Unity: Our Adventure: The Focolare Movement. Brooklyn, N.Y.: New City Press, 1987.

Whitehead, Evelyn E., and James D. Whitehead. *Christian Life Patterns: The Psychological Challenges and Religious Invitations of Adult Life.* New York: Crossroad, 1992.

————. *Seasons of Strength: New Visions of Adult Christian Maturing.* Garden City, N.Y.: Doubleday, 1984.

Williams, Charles. *Descent into Hell.* Grand Rapids: William B. Eerdmans, 1987.

————. *He Came Down from Heaven.* Grand Rapids: William B. Eerdmans, 1984.

Winter, Miriam Therese. *WomanPrayer, WomanSong: Resources for Ritual, Liturgies, Songs.* New York: Crossroad, 1987.

————. *WomanWisdom: A Feminist Lectionary and Psalter on Women of the Hebrew Scriptures,* Part I. New York: Crossroad, 1991.

————. *WomanWitness: A Feminist Lectionary and Psalter on Women of the Hebrew Scriptures,* Part II. New York: Crossroad, 1991.

————. *WomanWord: A Feminist Lectionary and Psalter on Women of the New Testament.* New York: Crossroad, 1990.

Wren, Brian. *What Language Shall I Borrow? God-Talk in Worship: A Male Response to Feminist Theology.* New York: Crossroad, 1990.

Wuellner, Flora S. *Prayer and Our Bodies.* Nashville: Upper Room, 1987.

The Year of Grace of the Lord. Translated from the French by Deborah Cowen. Crestwood, N.Y.: St. Vladimir's Seminary Press, 1980.

156

A Partial List
of Retreat Centers

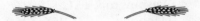

Bethabara
3767 64th Street
Holland, Michigan 49423
Telephone: (616) 857-7010

MorningStar Adventures
Route 1, 13 Mile Road
LeRoy, Michigan 49655
Telephone: (616) 768-4368 or 768-4869

Saint Gregory's Abbey
56500 Abbey Road
Three Rivers, Michigan 49093
Telephone: (616) 244-5893

Springbank Dominican Retreat Center
Route 2, Box 180
Kingstree, South Carolina 29556
Telephone: (803) 382-9777

COME TO THE FEAST

Columbiere Spirituality Center
9075 Big Lake Road
P.O. Box 139
Clarkston, Michigan 48347

Wellspring — Church of the Savior Retreat Center
11411 Neelsville Church Road
Germantown, Maryland 20876
Telephone: (301) 428-3373

Shalem Institute for Spiritual Formation
Mount St. Alban
Washington, D.C. 20016
Telephone: (202) 966-7050

Madonna House Retreat Center
220 C Street N.E.
Washington, D.C. 20002
Telephone: (202) 547-0177

The Resting Place
R.R. #1, Box 80
Mentone, Indiana 46539
Telephone: (219) 491-4082

Rune Hill
413 Halsey Valley Road
Spencer, New York 14883
Telephone: (607) 589-6392

Kirkridge Retreat and Study Center
Bangor, Pennsylvania 18013
Telephone: (215) 588-1793

The Hermitage
11321 Dutch Settlement Road
Three Rivers, Michigan 49093
Telephone: (616) 244-8696

A Partial List of Retreat Centers

Dominican Center at Marywood
2025 E. Fulton
Grand Rapids, Michigan 49503
Telephone: (616) 458-3966

Emmaus Monastery
7001 Tamarack
Vestaburg, Michigan 48891
Telephone: (517) 268-5494

Benedictine Abbey
Pecos, New Mexico 87552

Taize Community
71250 Cluny
France
Telephone: 85.50.30.02

Madonna House Apostolate
Combermere, Ontario
Canada KOJ ILO

The retreat centers I have listed above are places I have personally
visited or have heard about from a friend who had been there and
had a positive experience. Of course, there are literally hundreds
more retreat centers in this country and abroad. The book *A Guide
to Monastic Guest Houses* by J. Robert Beagle is a good resource
to consult. Also, the Catholic newspaper *National Catholic Reporter* has many advertisements for retreat centers in it, as does
the magazine *Praying*. Most Catholic churches have these and
other resources on hand. In addition, Retreats International offers,
for a small fee, a listing of over 500 retreat centers in the United
States and Canada; you can write or call (Retreats International,
Box 1067, Notre Dame, Indiana 46556, tel. 219-631-5320). Calling or writing to these centers requesting brochures and/or other
information will help you choose a place that is convenient and
seems best suited to your needs.

I have found that regular monthly visits to a retreat center are invaluable as a way of staying centered in and open to God. I have also met marvelous people at these special places, so that I now feel I am in a network of spiritually supportive soul-friends to whom I can turn and to whom I can go when the going gets rough.

My prayer is that you will find the same kind of support for yourself!